# File Management Made Simple, Windows Edition

Joseph Moran

D0263414

Apress®

**File Management Made Simple, Windows Edition**

ISBN-13 (pbk): 978-1-4842-1083-3

ISBN-13 (electronic): 978-1-4842-1082-6

Managing Director: Welmoed Spahr
Lead Editor: Steve Weiss, Jeffrey Pepper
Development Editor: James Markham
Technical Reviewer: Ronald Pacchiano
Editorial Board: Steve Anglin, Gary Cornell, Louise Corrigan, James T. DeWolf, Jonathan Gennick, Robert Hutchinson, Michelle Lowman, James Markham, Matthew Moodie, Susan McDermott, Jeffrey Pepper, Douglas Pundick, Dominic Shakeshaft, Gwenan Spearing, Matt Wade, Steve Weiss
Coordinating Editor: Melissa Maldonado
Copy Editor: Laura Lawrie
Compositor: SPi Global
Indexer: SPi Global
Artist: SPi Global

Distributed to the book trade worldwide b̲ 233 Spring Street, 6th Floor, New York, NY e-mail orders-ny@springer-sbm.com, or v and the sole member (owner) is Springer S SSBM Finance Inc is a **Delaware** corporatic

For information on translations, please e-

Apress and friends of ED books may be pu use. eBook versions and licenses are also our Special Bulk Sales–eBook Licensing w

Any source code or other supplementary to readers at www.apress.com. For detailed go to www.apress.com/source-code/.

# Contents at a Glance

# Contents

# About the Author

**Joseph Moran** first caught the computer bug from an Atari 800 given as a Christmas gift by his Mom in 1979. That eventually led to over two decades of writing countless articles for numerous Web and print publications (back when print was a still a thing), as well as coauthoring two previous books on Windows.

These days, when not writing he spends his days doing IT consulting and support.

# About the Technical Reviewer

**Ronald V. Pacchiano** has worked as technical writer and product reviewer for over 20 years. He is an accomplished technology journalist, having written for publications such as *Windows Sources, Computer Shopper* and *PC Magazine*, where he has produced product reviews, how-to guides, and in-depth feature stories. He also spent several years working as a columnist for *Practically Networked* and *Small Business Computing*, writing video game reviews for CNET, and he spent several years working in public relations, focusing on the technology sector.

Beyond publishing , Ron works in the IT field where he functions as a systems integrator and technology specialist with expertise in Windows server management, desktop support, and network administration.

Today Ron works as a systems analyst for a New Jersey–based pharmaceutical company. When not hip-deep in service requests, he often spends his time evaluating new technologies and working on various projects.

He resides in New York with his wife Jessica and their two cats, Frankie and Phoebe.

# Acknowledgments

Thanks to all the folks at Apress for their guidance in seeing this project through to completion, as well as to Ron Pacchiano for lending his watchful eye to the technical aspects of this book. Most of all, thanks to my wife and daughter for tolerating—indeed, sharing in—my near-obsession with all kinds of technology.

—Joseph Moran

# Introduction

Thanks for buying *File Management Made Simple, Windows Edition*. This book is for anyone who wants to learn how to take control of how files are created, organized, utilized, secured, and backed up on a PC.

I've tried to keep jargon to a minimum, so you don't need to be a tech expert to benefit from this book. Within these pages you'll find information that applies to the two most recent versions of Windows—Windows 8.1 as well as Windows 10, which was released while this book was being written.

## What You'll Learn

Chapter 1, Let's Go Exploring, looks at the anatomy and features of File Explorer, Windows' built-in file management tool. This chapter also outlines the standard set of folders that Windows provides for storage of different kinds of files.

Chapter 2, Working with Files, explains the difference between files and folders and how each can be named. This chapter also covers some basic file management tasks, including how to select files or folders and how to copy, move, or rename them.

Chapter 3, Keeping Files and Folders Organized, explains how to use Libraries to keep track of files and folders stored in different places on a PC. It also includes tips on how to best to download and open files from websites and email, and how to ensure work file changes aren't lost when an application crashes.

Chapter 4, Managing and Protecting Files with User Accounts, discusses the different types of user accounts available in Windows, and why it's important that each user of a PC has his or her own user account (as opposed to everyone sharing one acount).

Chapter 5, Managing and Reclaiming Disk Space, explores why your PC might run low on disk space, how to determine how disk space is being used, and how to free up disk space.

Chapter 6, Working with File Types and Programs (Apps), looks at file extensions and how they're used to determine what program a file will open in. This chapter also shows how to change the default program that opens a particular type of file.

Chapter 7, Searching for Files, is a detailed look at Windows' file search capability, which can allow you to efficiently find a file you're looking for via keyword, date, type, and other characteristics.

Chapter 8, Cloud Storage and Transporting Files, looks at how online storage can allow you to augment the storage capacity of your PC, synchronize files across multiple PCs, and share large files that are not easily shared by other means (e.g., via email). This chapter also looks at more conventional ways of moving files from Point A to Point B, such as USB storage devices and optical (DVD or Blu-ray) discs.

Chapter 9, Managing Open Files and Windows, explores ways to keep frequently used files close at hand, such as by pinning them to the taskbar. This chapter also highlights ways to work efficiently with multiple files at the same time by easily switching between open files or displaying up to four files on screen simultaneously.

Chapter 10, Sharing Files on a Home Network, shows how to share files across mulitple Windows PCs via a network, including setting up a HomeGroup, connecting USB storage to your Wi-Fi router, or adding a home server to your network.

Chapter 11, Backing Up Your Files, explains how to protect your files from loss or damage by backing them up to an external hard drive using Windows' File History feature. It also discusses alternative backup methods, including backing up to a remote server via an online service.

Chapter 12, Keeping Your Personal Data Secure via Encryption, discusses Windows' encryption features Device Encryption and BitLocker, as well as third-party options that can ensure that your files are protected against unauthorized access in the event that your PC is lost or stolen.

Chapter 13, Transfer Your Files to a New PC, outlines various options to get files from a PC running an older version of Windows to one with a newer version, including File History, Windows Easy Transfer, and third-party tools.

Chapter 14, Properly Disposing of an Old PC, outlines the steps that you should take before selling, donating, or otherwise disposing of a PC to ensure that no one will be able to recover and view the personal files you once had stored on it.

# CHAPTER 1

■ ■ ■

# Let's Go Exploring

The cornerstone of file management in Windows is the built-in File Explorer utility, which packs a lot of information and features into a relatively compact space. It often is the first place to go when you want to work with files and folders on your PC or on any of the devices that are connected to your PC.

In this chapter, we'll go over the geography of a File Explorer window and how the different parts are used. In later chapters, we'll be delving into some of File Explorer's features in greater detail.

## Anatomy of a File Explorer Window

You'll find File Explorer's icon (it looks like a folder) in the Windows Taskbar at the bottom of the screen. You'll also find File Explorer listed in the menu when you right click or long tap the Windows logo in the lower left corner of the screen (Figure 1-1).

1

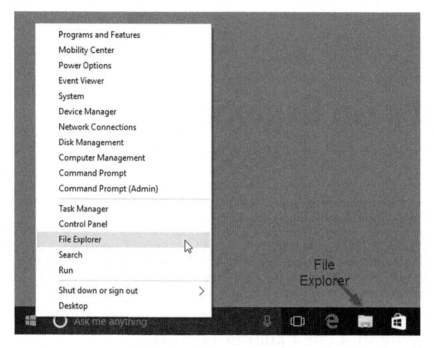

**Figure 1-1.** *Two ways to access File Explorer*

When File Explorer opens, you'll see a window that looks a lot like the one shown in Figure 1-2.

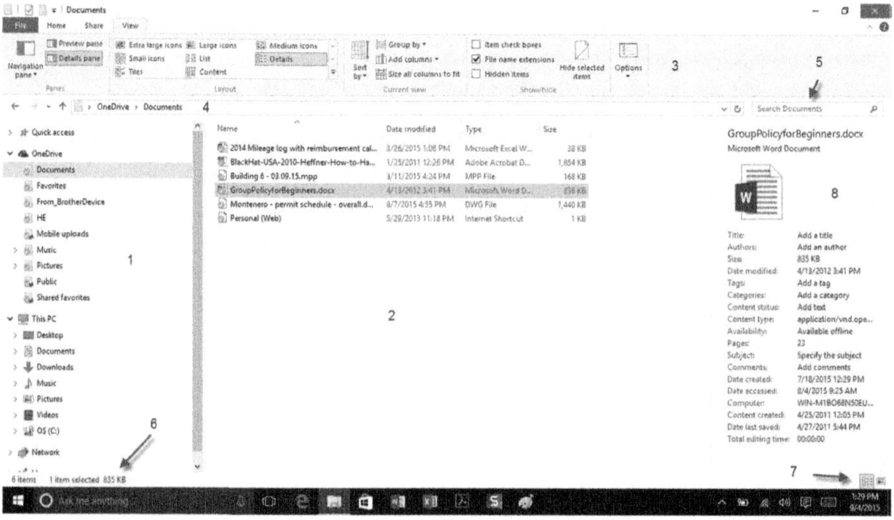

**Figure 1-2.** *Parts of a (Windows 10) File Explorer window*

## Navigation Pane

This is where you choose the location that you want to access. This may include folders stored directly on your PC or on devices that are connected to your PC, such as external storage devices or networked folders. Tap or click an item to select it, or tap or click the arrow next to an item to expand it.

## Contents Pane

When you select a folder item in the navigation pane, you'll see the contents of that folder displayed in the contents pane. Depending on how File Explorer's view is configured, the right pane may display the contents of the selected location using variable-sized icons or as a list with column headings that show file details.

## Ribbon

Here you'll find a set of tabs labeled File, Home, Share, and View, which provide access to common operations or tasks that you can perform on a selected item or items. The tab selected and options displayed in the ribbon will often change depending on the location or type of file or folder selected.

---

If you don't see the Ribbon, click the downward-pointing arrowhead near the upper right of the File Explorer window. When the Ribbon is visible this changes to point upward, allowing you to rehide the Ribbon.

---

## Address Bar

This displays the path to your current location. Click or tap part of the path to jump to that specific location, or use the arrow keys to the left (Back, Forward, and Up) to navigate instead. You can also type in a new location here.

## Search Box

Enter a word or phrase (or part of one) here to search for it in the selected location. (For more on searching, see Chapter 7, Searching for Files.)

## Status Bar

Displays the number of items in a location, or the number and size of items selected.

# View Options

These two buttons, located at the lower right corner of the File Explorer window, let you easily switch the layout of the contents pane between the aforementioned details (left button) and large icons (right button) views.

---

## MORE VIEW OPTIONS

The View tab (shown in Figure 1-2) gives you myriad additional options to customize how the contents of the selected folder are displayed.

Also, when viewing the contents of a folder in the Details view, as shown, clicking on a column heading (Name, Date, Type, Etc.) will sort the column alternately in ascending or decending order. In addition, by right clicking or long tapping a column heading, you can display additional headings or remove existing ones by adding or removing a check mark from the items that you want (Figure 1-3).

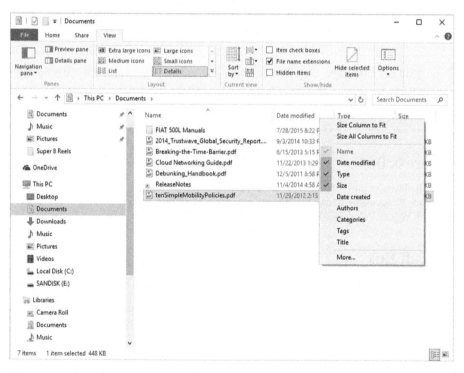

***Figure 1-3.*** *Customizing File Explorer's Details view*

## Preview/Details Pane

When a file is selected, this displays either properties of the selected file (details pane) or lets you view the contents of the file without having to open it first (preview pane).

---

The details/preview pane is not visible by default. To display it, select the View tab in the Ribbon and tap or click either Details Pane or Preview Pane (see Figure 1-3). Notice that both panes can't be active at the same time.

---

Now that we've gone over the anatomy of a File Explorer window, let's run down the locations that you're likely to encounter in the Navigation pane.

# This PC

Here you'll find a collection of folders that reside on your PC that are intended to help you store and organize different types of files. Programs will typically use these folders as default locations to store the files that they create.

## Desktop

This represents files and folders you place on your Desktop—that is, atop the background wallpaper you see on your screen.

## Documents

A place to store files created in programs such as Microsoft Word, Microsoft Excel, and similar programs.

## Downloads

The default storage location for files downloaded from the Internet (typically via a Web browser such as Internet Explorer or Google Chrome).

## Music

A place for music and other audio files. Music programs such as iTunes and similar programs store their files here.

## Pictures

A place for digital photos and other graphics images.

## Videos

A place for video files.

## OS/Local Disk C:

Typically labeled either "OS" or "Local Disk" C:, this represents your PC's internal storage. You can access the Windows operating system and program files from here, as well as all of the file storage locations just outlined (more on this later in this chapter). However, in the course of normal file management, you generally won't need to get to your file storage folders this way because they're accessible elsewhere in This PC.

---

If you have any external/removable storage devices such as USB Flash/hard drives or optical disc drives (DVD/Blu-Ray), you'll see them listed under This PC along with a drive letter label (often D: or E:). Notice that you won't see an optical drive appear in the Navigation pane unless there's a disc inserted, but if you highlight This PC, the optical drive will appear in the Contents pane whether there's a disc inserted or not.

---

# Private versus Public Folders

Each person with a Windows user account on the PC gets his or her own personal set of the storage folders described earlier. As shown in Figure 1-4, these folders are located in the Users folder within a folder named after the account. Under normal circumstances, the contents of these folders are off limits to other users of the PC unless you explicitly choose to share them, although another user with an Adminstrator account on the PC can also gain access to any other user's files. For more on User Accounts, see Chapter 4, Managing and Protecting Files with User Accounts.

In Figure 1-4, you'll also notice another set of folders labeled "Public," which largely mirror the set of user's personal/private folders (all but Desktop). As the name implies, these public folders are accessible by all users of the PC, so they're a good place to put a file (or a copy of a file) when you want another user of the PC to be able to access it.

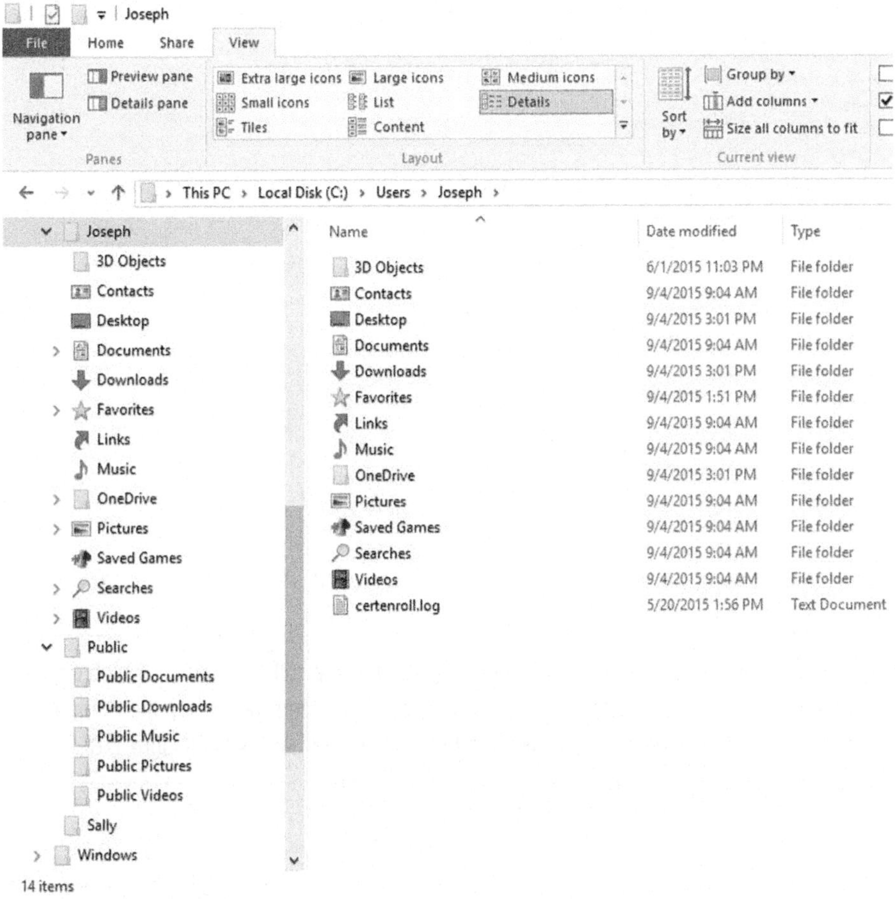

*Figure 1-4. File Explorer view of a user's storage folders, along with the Public folders*

Aside from the items listed under This PC, File Explorer's Navigation pane will also provide access to files and folders found in other locations (not all of which are visible in Figure 1-2).

# Quick Access

This is a feature in Windows 10 that provides convenient access to frequently used folders. Windows automatically puts some folders in Quick access for you, but you can add your own as well. As shown in Figure 1-5, to add a folder to Quick access right click or long tap a folder and choose Pin to Quick access.

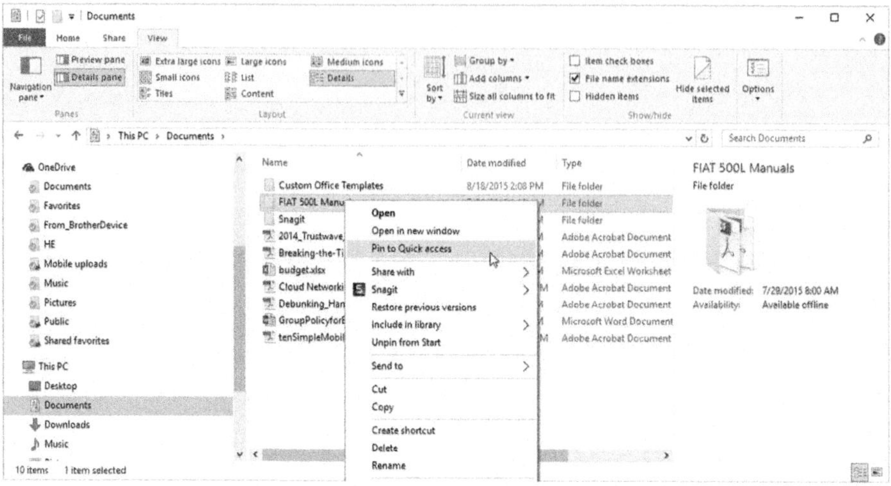

***Figure 1-5.*** *Adding a folder to Quick access in Windows 10*

Instead of Quick access, Windows 8.1 uses a similar feature called Favorites, which works a bit differently. To add a folder to Favorites, select the folder, then click or tap the Home tab, select the Easy Access button, and choose Add to Favorites from the list (Figure 1-6).

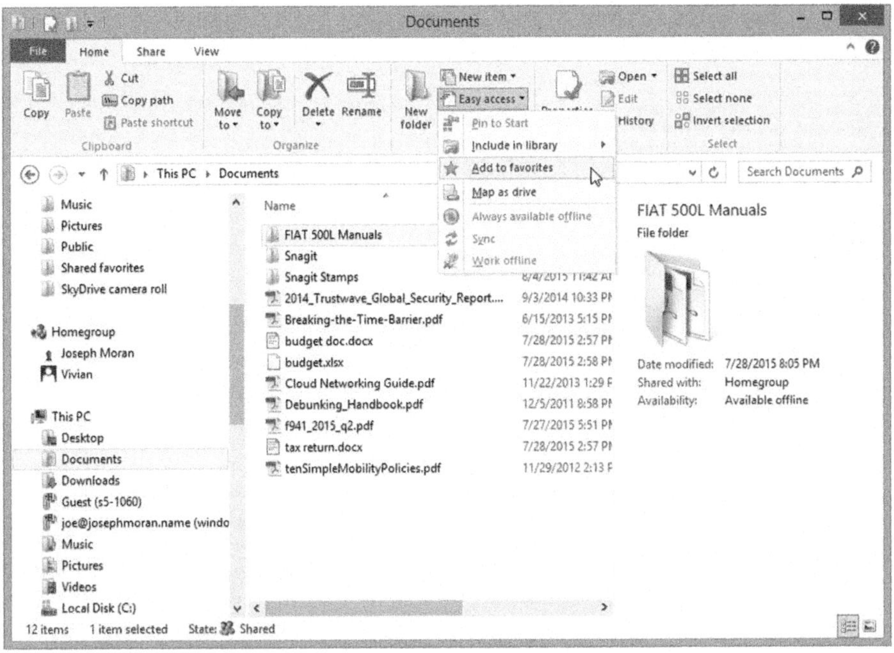

***Figure 1-6.*** *Adding a folder to favorites in Windows 8.1*

Once you've added a folder to Quick access/Favorites (and it's worth noting you can only add folders, not files), those locations are a quick click or tap away under the appropriate heading at the top of File Explorer's Navigation pane. In either Windows 10 or Windows 8.1, click on a folder under Quick access/Favorites in the Navigation pane and you'll see the contents of that folder to the right in the Contents pane. In Windows 10, click on the Quick access heading itself and you'll see a list of files and folders you recently used, even if you didn't explicitly add the folders to Quick access (Figure 1-7).

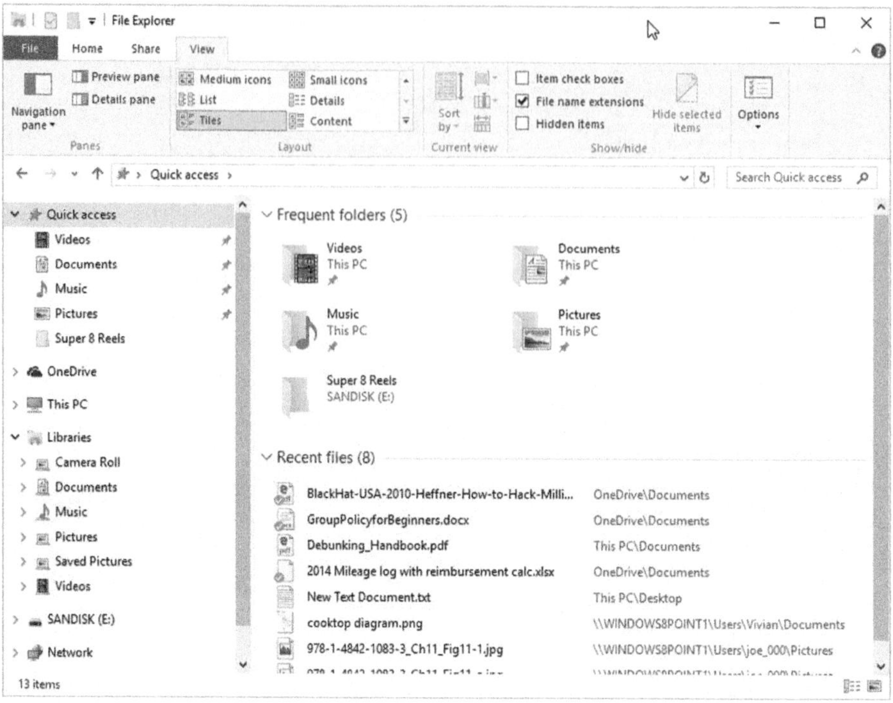

*Figure 1-7.* *Quick access to files and folders in Windows 10*

# OneDrive

OneDrive is Microsoft's cloud (online) storage service, which is integrated into Windows. Files and folders that you've stored on OneDrive and synced to your PC will appear here. (For more on OneDrive and cloud storage, see Chapter 8, Cloud Storage and Transporting Files.)

# Network

This area will display other PCs or devices with storage capabilities (such as NAS devices) that are connected to the same network as your PC.

# HomeGroup

A HomeGroup is a network of Windows PCs that can share files and other resources. If you've created or joined a HomeGroup, other members of the HomeGroup will appear here. (For more on HomeGroups and other methods of sharing files on a network, see Chapter 10, Sharing Files over a Home Network.)

# Libraries

Libraries are a handy feature of Windows. They're essentially "virtual folders" that give you a way to manage folders located in multiple locations all from a single location. We'll cover Libraries in more detail in Chapter 3, Organizing Your Files, but for now it's important to note that Libraries don't appear by default in either Windows 8.1 or Windows 10, so if you want to see and use them you have to turn them on first.

To have Libraries appear in File Explorer's Navigation pane for either version of Windows, click or tap the View tab, then select the button labeled Navigation pane and select Show libraries as shown in Figure 1-8.

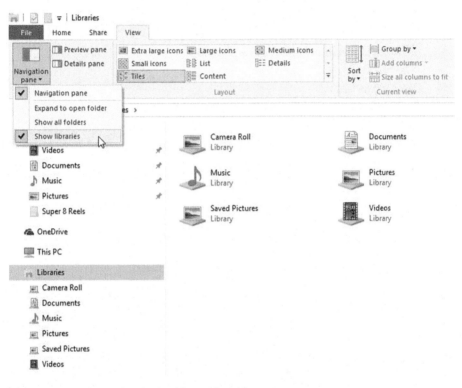

***Figure 1-8.*** *Making Libraries visible in File Explorer*

## WHERE DOES FILE EXPLORER AUTOMATICALLY OPEN?

This depends on a couple of variables. In Windows 8.1, File Explorer automatically opens with This PC highlighted by default.

In Windows 10, File Explorer always opens with Quick Access highlighted, although you can change it to This PC instead. To make File Explorer open with This PC highlighted, click or tap the File tab and select "Change folder and search options." Finally, tap or click the "Open File Explorer to" box at the top of the window and select "This PC" as shown in Figure 1-9. The change will take effect the next time you open File Explorer.

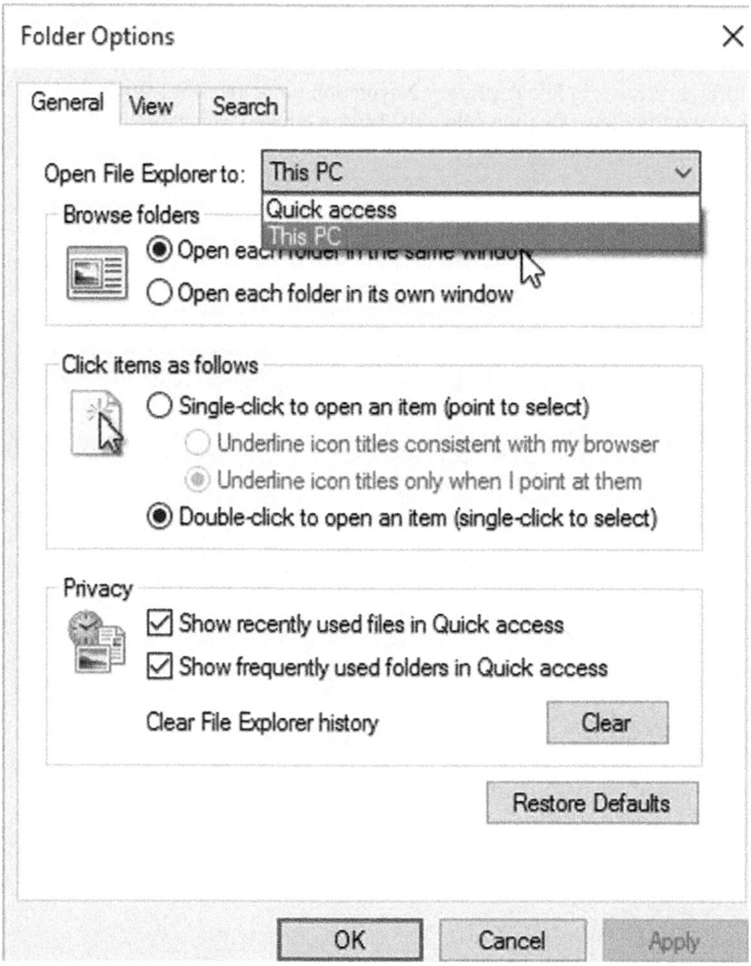

*Figure 1-9.* *Changing File Explorer to open in This PC instead of Quick access (Windows 10)*

Notice the additional options under the "Privacy" heading in Figure 1-9, which allow you to disable the automatic display of recently used files and frequently used folders (i.e., those you used but didn't explicitly add to Quick access).

**CHAPTER 2**

■ ■ ■

# Working with Files

Now that we've had a tour of File Explorer, we'll delve into some ways to use it to manage files and folders, as well as how to perform common tasks such as renaming, copying, and moving items.

## What Are Files?

Simply put, a file is container that holds a particular kind of information, such as an image, a song, or a document. In Windows, every file has a name and an extension (extensions are usually three characters, but it could be two or four) separated by a period, for example, *family budget.xlsx*.

A file extension tells you what kind of information a file contains and, thus, what kind of program will open it. In this example, the xlsx extension denotes the file can be opened with Microsoft's Excel spreadsheet software or another compatible program.

It's important to note that Windows normally hides file extensions from view in File Explorer, and although you can make those extension visible by putting a check in the File name extension box found under File Explorer's View menu, you generally won't need to do that because, as shown in Figure 2-1, when File Explorer's Details view is selected, the Type column will tell you what kind of files are displayed.

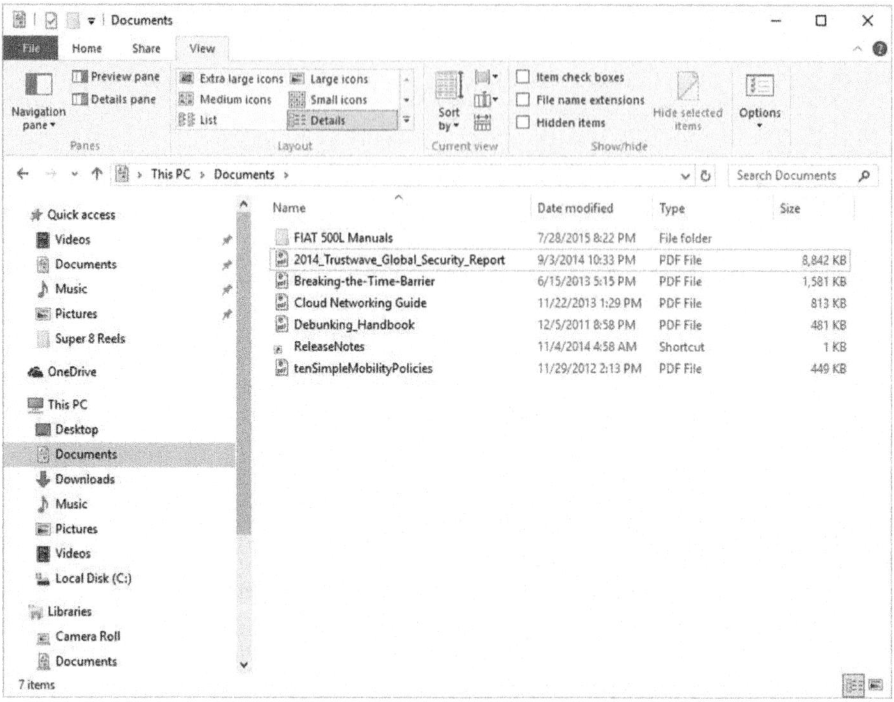

**Figure 2-1.** *File Explorer's Type column tells you what type of file you're looking at, even when file extensions aren't visible*

---

For more on file extensions and how they determine what program will open a file, see Chapter 6.

---

# What Are folders?

Wheras a file is a container for information, a folder is a container for files. Folders help keep your files organized, and as we mentioned in the previous chapter, Windows automatically sets up several standard folders—Documents, Music, Pictures, and Video—for you to store various kinds of files.

Although you're free to store files (almost) anywhere you want on a PC, a basic tenet of good file management is to always keep your files in one of these four folders, or in subfolders located within one these folders.

## WHAT ABOUT THE DESKTOP?

The Desktop is another one of the standard folders we learned about in the previous chapter, and if you're like many Windows users, you've developed a habit of saving files on the Desktop in order to keep them within easy reach.

The problem is that while "working off the Desktop" may seem expedient at first, over time it almost always leads to chaos. As more and more stuff gets saved to the Desktop, it becomes harder and harder to quickly find the item you want among the dozens or scores of identical-looking file and folder icons that litter it.

Bottom line—you should resist the temptation to use the Desktop as a catchall "junk drawer." There are several ways to keep frequently used files close at hand in Windows, including a Search feature and Pinned Items/Jump Lists. Read more about them in Chapters 7 and 9, respectively.

# Creating a New Folder/Subfolder

There are two main ways to create a new folder or subfolder in File Explorer. After navigating to the location where you want the new folder, right click or long tap in the blank space of the Contents Pane (i.e., not atop an existing filze or folder), select New, then Folder. The other option is to click or tap the Home menu's New folder button (Figure 2-2).

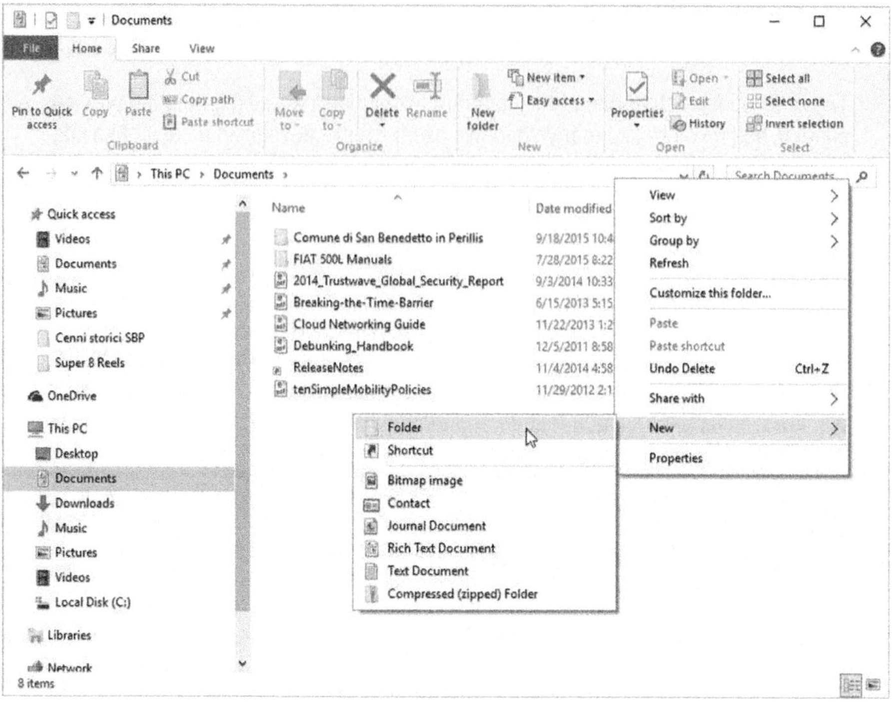

**Figure 2-2.** *Create a new folder via the New folder button, or by right-clicking/long tapping empty space in the Contents Pane*

Whichever of these options you choose, you'll see a new folder listing with the label "New Folder" highlighted (Figure 2-3). To name the folder something more meaningful, simply start typing (you don't have to position the mouse cursor or backspace over the "New folder" label first).

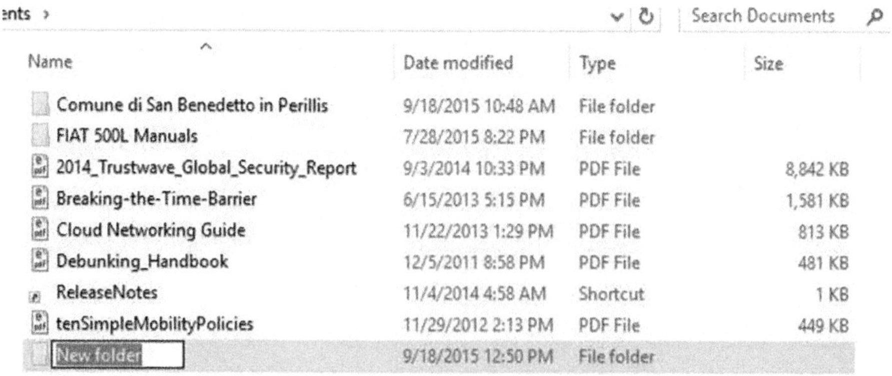

**Figure 2-3.** *To name your new folder, just type over the highlighted "New Folder" label*

# Selecting Multiple Files and Folders

You already know that you can select a file or folder by clicking or tapping on it. When it comes to selecting multiple files or folders, by contrast, you have several different options to choose from.

## Option 1: Use SHIFT and CTRL with the mouse

To select multiple adjacent files or folders, click or tap the first item you want so that it's highlighted, then hold down Shift and click or tap the last file you want. The first item, last item, and all the items in between will be highlighted (Figure 2-4).

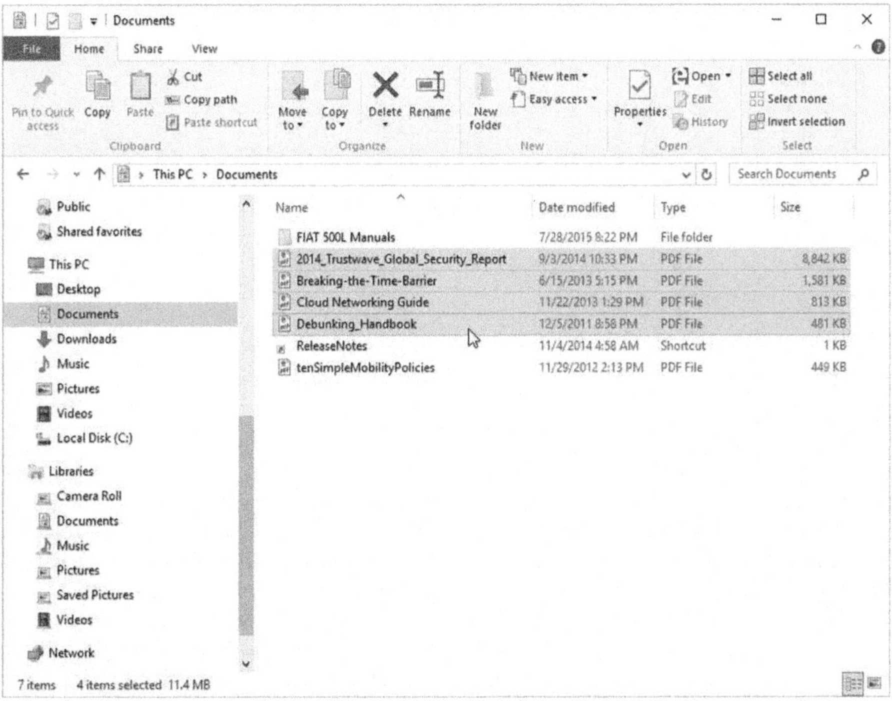

***Figure 2-4.*** *Use the mouse (or your finger) and the Shift key to select a range of consecutive files (or the Home menu's Select all button to select all of them)*

---

To select all items, use the Select all option under the Home menu, or press CTRL+A.

---

To select multiple files that **are not** adjacent, click or tap the first item you want, then hold down CTRL as you click or tap additional items. This will allow you to select only specific items of interest, as shown in Figure 2-5.

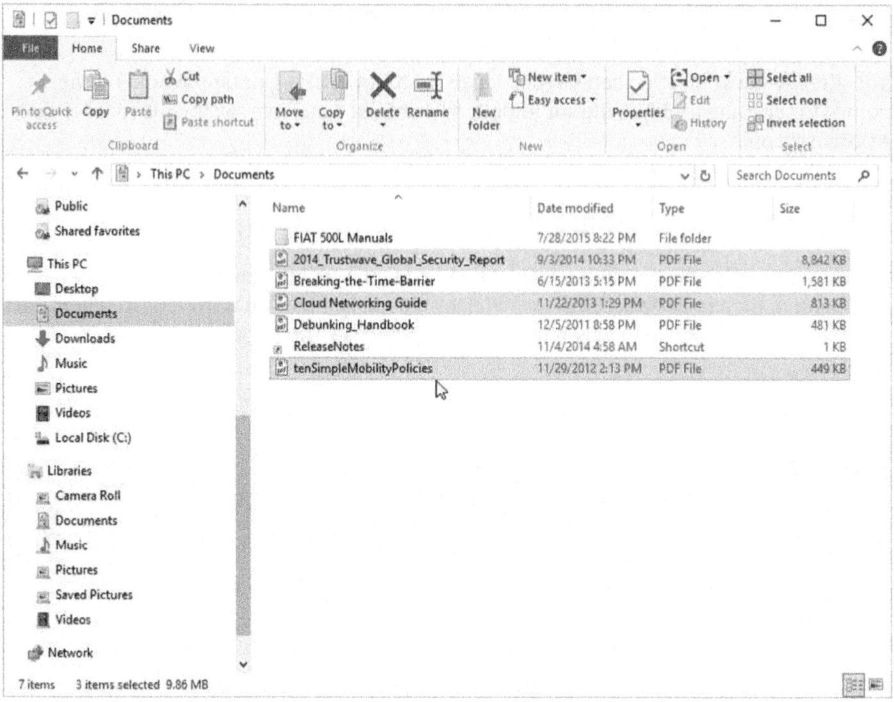

***Figure 2-5.*** *Use the mouse (or your finger) and the CTRL key to select individual nonadjacent files*

# Option 2: Use item check boxes

An alternate way to select multiple items (and, indeed, the only practical way if you're using a PC that lacks a keyboard or pointing device) is to use File Explorer's item check boxes. Item check boxes may already be activated if your PC is touch-enabled, but if not you can turn it on by (naturally) checking the box labeled Item check boxes in the View menu

When you turn on item check boxes and have File Explorer set to Details view, a narrow column of empty space with a check box at the top will be visible along the left edge of the contents pane (Figure 2-6). To select a file, hover the mouse in this space next to an item; you'll see a check box appear, which you can click to select the item. (The check box at the top of this column is used to Select all.)

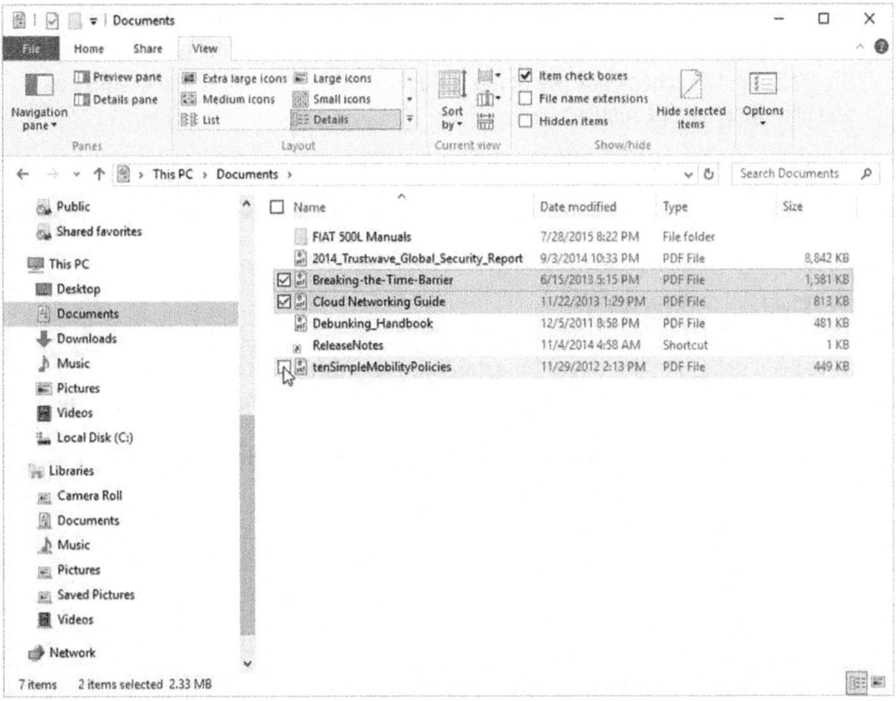

***Figure 2-6.*** *With Item check boxes turned on, click or tap the check box column to select individual files*

Keep in mind that when you want to select most of the items in a list but not all of them, it can often be quicker and easier to Select all first and then unselect the items you don't want rather than individually select all the items you do want.

## SELECTING MULTIPLE ITEMS VIA TAPPING

Selecting multiple file check boxes by tapping alone (i.e., without a mouse or other pointing device) can be quite tricky. Tap on the blank space column next to an item to expose and check the item's box, but be careful—because it's a relatively narrow space, it's quite easy to accidently tap the item itself (thus highlighting it) or to unselect an item when you're trying to select an adjacent one.

You might be tempted to switch File Explorer to a different view (e.g., Large Icon, in order to make items bigger and easier to tap), but it can still be difficult to hone in on the location of the check box (it's at the upper left) without exposing it in advance as you can when using a mouse.

However imperfect, Details view is still your best bet when you want to select multiple files using only a finger, but it can take some practice to become proficient.

# File/Folder Names

If you've been using a PC for a very long time, you may recall that many years ago file (and folder) names were limited to eight characters. That's no longer the case, but there are still some practical limitations to be aware of.

First, a handful of characters are invalid for use in a file/folder name (see Table 2-1).

***Table 2-1.*** *Invalid file name characters*

| | |
|---|---|
| Backslash and forward slash | \ / |
| Greater than and less than | >< |
| Question Mark | ? |
| Colon | : |
| Asterisk | * |
| Quotation Mark | " |
| Vertical bar (on most keyboards this is on the same key as the backslash) | \| |

Second, although there's a maximum of 255 characters that can be in any individual file or folder name, the more practical limitation to be aware of in Windows is that the complete path to a file should contain no more than 260 characters.

The complete path to a file is the file name plus the names of all the folders and subfolders that lead to it, including spaces, and when this exceeds 260 characters, Windows will likely display a (vague and uninformative) error message when you try to copy, move, delete, or even open the file. For this reason, it's a good idea to keep file and folder names as succinct as possible in order to steer clear of this 260 character limit.

So for example, the path:

> *c:\Users\Joseph\Documents\Book Chapters\Chapter 2 – Working with Files\Chapter 2.docx*

contains more than 80 characters, which is admittedly well under 260 characters.

But while 260 characters seem like a lot, and it is, under certain circumstances exceeding the limit can be easier than you think. For example, if we had used the full name of this book in the folder and file names of this path:

> **c:\Users\Joseph\Documents\File Management Made Simple, Windows Edition**
>
> **Book Chapters\File Management Made Simple, Windows Edition**
>
> **Chapter 2 – Working with Files\File Management Made Simple, Windows Edition Chapter 2.docx**

the length of the path almost triples to well over 200 characters. It's also worth noting that it's possible to run up against the 260 character threshold when attempting to copy or move a file from a location with a short path to one with a longer path.

In a nutshell, to avoid potential problems caused by exceeding the 260 character path limit, avoid unnecessary repetition and verbosity when naming files and folders.

# Renaming Items

There are several easy ways to rename a file or folder. Once you've selected an item you want to rename, one method is to right click or long tap the item and choose Rename. Another is to select the file and press F2 or use the Rename button found within File Explorer's Home menu (Figure 2-7). In all cases, the existing name will be highlighted and ready to be typed over with a new one, just like we showed in Figure 2-3.

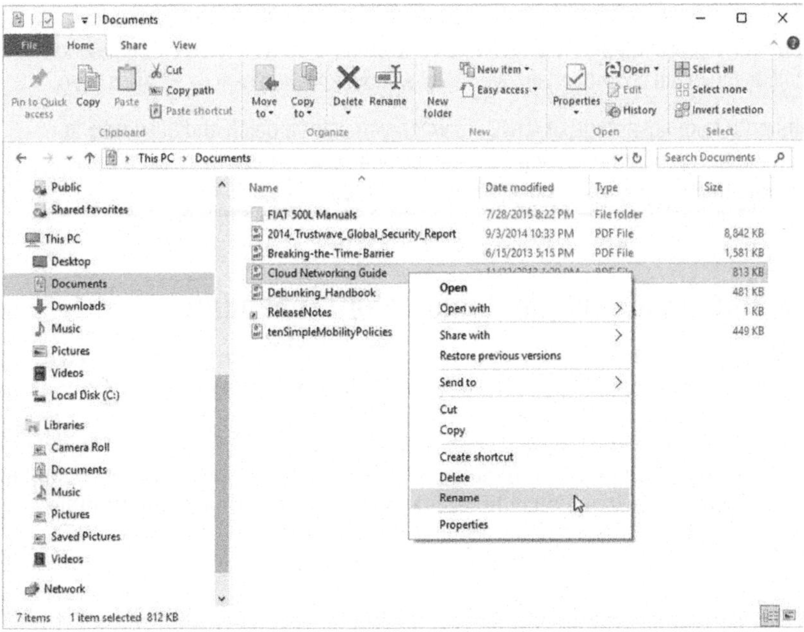

**Figure 2-7.**  *Rename an item via the Rename button or right-click/long tap menu (or press F2)*

# Renaming Multiple Files and Folders

There may be times when you find yourself needing to rename multiple files and/or folders rather than just one. This often is referred to as batch renaming. There are several methods for doing this, and which one is best depends on how many items you're dealing with and how you want to rename them.

## Option 1: Switch between items with the Tab key

If you want to rename a handful of items in a folder, but not all with similar or serial names, you can make this task easier by renaming the first item as we just described. However, after typing in the new name, press Tab instead of Enter. This will jump to the file below, which will be highlighted and ready for renaming. Repeat this process as necessary until you've renamed all the files you need to, finally pressing Enter at the last one.

There are a few things to keep in mind about renaming files this way. First, if you need to go back up in your list, you can use use Shift + Tab. Second, if you make a mistake while typing a new name, press Ctrl+Z to undo your changes and start over (for that file, not the entire renaming process).

---

### THE MANY USES OF CTRL + Z

This seems like a good time to highlight the importance and usefulness of the CTRL +Z command. Also known as "Undo" and supported in most areas of Windows—and in most Windows programs—CTRL + Z reverses the last action you took, and depending on the situation can be either a convenience or a godsend (particularly if you did something inadvertently without knowing exactly what or how).

Remember to take advantage of CTRL +Z when you want a quick and easy way to roll back the last thing you did. And if you do so and realize maybe you were OK with the change after all, may we suggest CTRL + Y (Redo).

---

## Option 2: Highlight multiple items before renaming

Let's say you have a large number of files that you want to rename in the same way. For example, a folder full of images with undescriptive names from a vacation you just took, but you want to name them all "Summer Vacation 2015."

To do this, select all of the files that you want to rename, then press F2. The first file you selected will be highlighted for renaming; type your new name and press Enter, and each file will be renamed with an incrementing number in parentheses—for example, Summer Vacation 2015 (1), Summer Vacation 2015 (2), and so on.

## Option 3: Use third-party software

If you need to rename files with more speed and/or flexibility than the first two methods offer, Windows doesn't offer an easy way to do it. But as is often the case in such situations, third-party software can do the job.

In particular, we recommend trying a free utility called Advanced Renamer, which you can download from www.advancedrenamer.com. With it, you can do things such as remove or insert only certain text from a file name, change the case of characters, renumber files, and more. Even better, it allows you to simulate a lengthy or complex renaming task before you perform it so that you can be sure that the result will be what you expect.

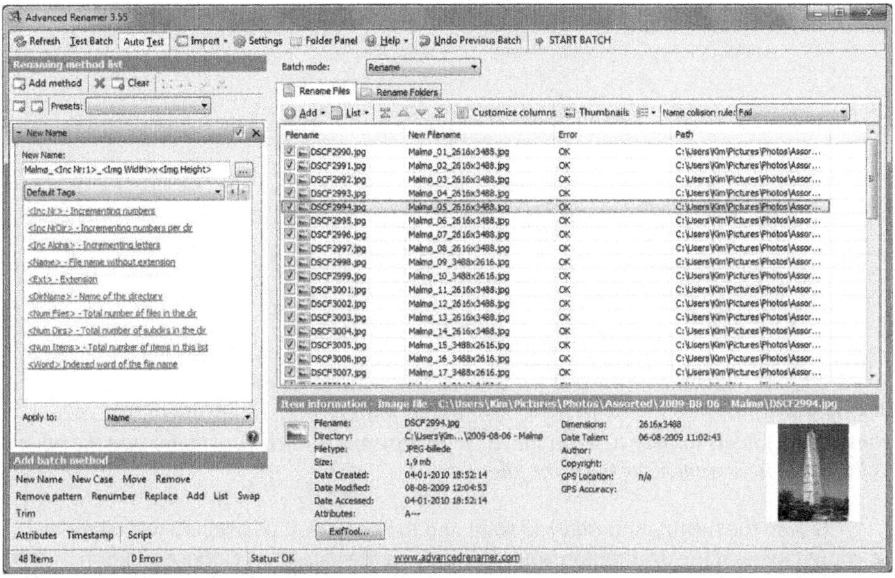

*Figure 2-8. Advanced Renamer lets you batch rename files in powerful and flexbile ways*

# Moving or Copying Items

There are many different ways to move or copy items in File Explorer, but we'll focus on two in particular.

## Option 1: Move to/Copy to buttons

One of the easiest ways to move/copy items in File Explorer is to use the buttons provided for that purpose. First select the item(s) that you're interested in, then click or tap on either the Move to or Copy to button found under the Home menu. In either case you'll see the same list of destinations (Figure 2-9), which includes your standard set of user folders as well as recently used folders (in Windows 8.1) or folders that you've pinned to Quick Access (Windows 10).

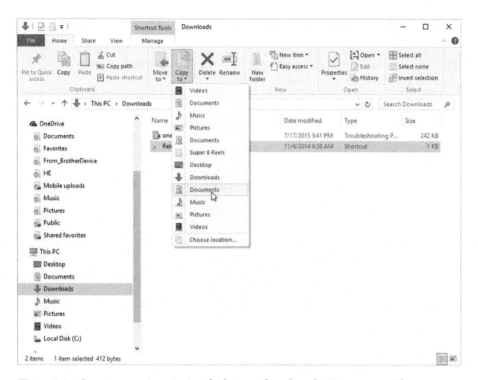

***Figure 2-9.*** *Copy or move items using the buttons found on the Home menu. The reason that certain folders appear twice in the list is because one is the actual folder and the other is the Quick Access entry for the same folder*

Click on the destination that you want and the items you've selected will be moved or copied there. If the destination you want isn't on the list, select Choose location (Figure 2-10) and then navigate to the desired location.

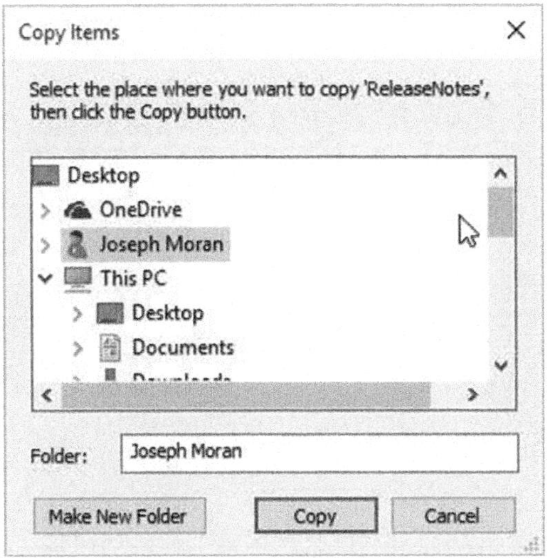

*Figure 2-10. Specify your own desitnation after using the Move to or Copy to buttons*

When you select items in File Explorer, the Home menu should appear by default, but if you've previously switched to a different menu, such as Share or View, you'll need to switch back to Home to access the Move to and Copy to buttons.

## Option 2: Cut/copy and paste

Another way to copy or move items—in File Explorer or elsewhere in Windows, such as the Desktop) is via Cut/Copy and Paste. To use this method, select the item(s) you want, then right click or long tap them. Choose Copy if you want to copy the item(s) or Cut if you want to move them. Then, navigate to your destination, right click or long tap on it (if you're selecting it in the navigation pane—in the contents pane, right click or long tap blank space instead), and then choose Paste to complete the copy/move process (Figures 2-11 and 2-12).

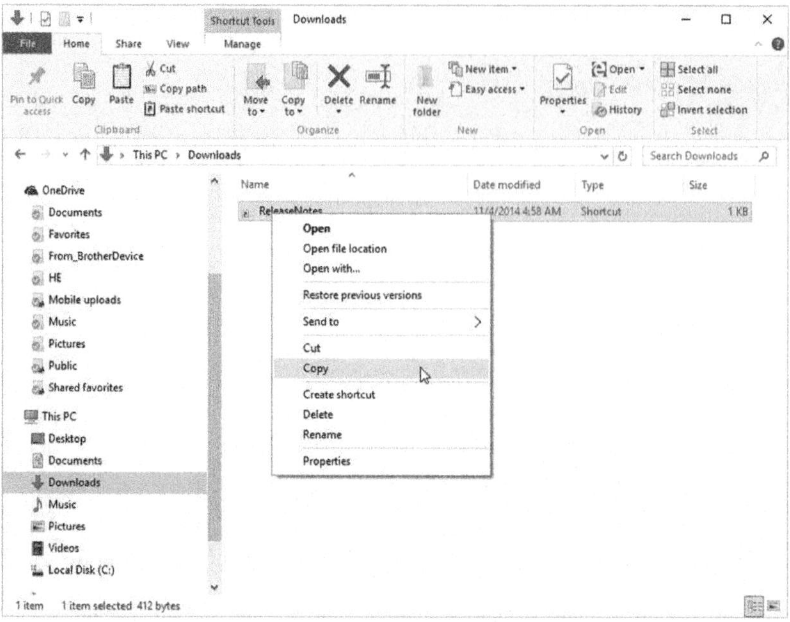

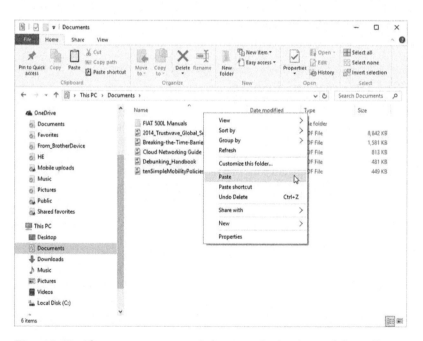

**Figure 2-11.** *Highlight an item, then right click or long tap and choose Copy or Cut (move)*

**Figure 2-12.** *After you cut or copy, switch to your destination and choose Paste to complete the process*

When copying or moving a large number of files and/or folders, you may find it helpful to have two File Explorer windows open at once (one open to the source folder, the other to the destination). An easy way to do this is right click or long tap your desination in File Explorer's Navigation (left) pane and choose Open in new window, as shown in Figure 2-13.

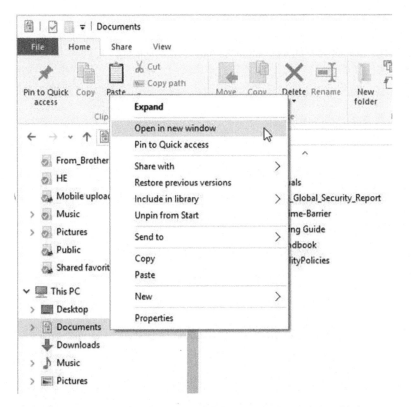

***Figure 2-13.*** *Keep both your source and destination locations visible by opening one of them in a new File Explorer window*

---

See Chapter 9 for a way to arrange two (or more) windows on screen so that they don't overlap.

---

# FILE TRANSFER PROGRESS WINDOW

Whenever you move or copy items, you'll see a window (like the one shown in Figure 2-14) that lets you monitor the progress of the transfer and when it's due to finish. (The exception is when you're transferring so little data that the process finishes in less than about a second.) You don't need to wait for a transfer to complete before starting another one, although keep in mind that if you perform too many transfers at once your PC's performance may slow noticeably.

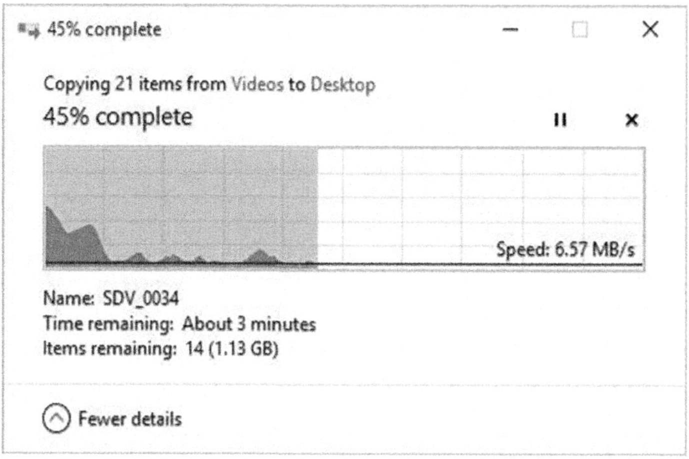

*Figure 2-14.* The status of a copy/move operation in progress

# CHAPTER 3

■ ■ ■

# Keeping Files and Folders Organized

In the first two chapters of this book, we covered the basics of File Explorer and how to use it to perform basic file management tasks. In this chapter, we'll look at how to use libraries to keep files and folders organized so that you'll always be able to find what you're looking for quickly and easily. Then we'll turn our attention to how to avoid "Where did my file go?" situations and other problems when performing common file-management tasks.

## Libraries

Libraries are a feature that Microsoft introduced way back in 2009 with Windows 7. The company has deemphasized (read: hidden it by default) it in subsequent versions of Windows, including Windows 8.1 and Windows 10, but we think it's useful enough to talk about it here.

To view Libraries in File Explorer, click or tap the View tab, then select the button labeled Navigation pane and select Show libraries (Figure 3-1).

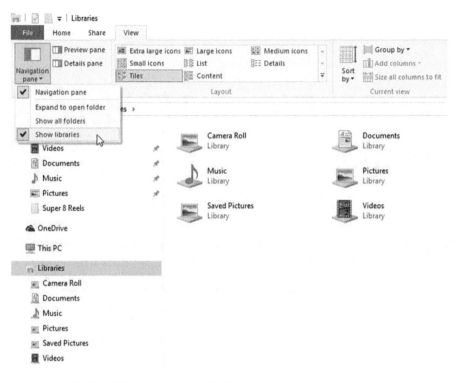

***Figure 3-1.*** *Making Libraries visible in File Explorer*

As we mentioned in Chapter 1, Libraries are basically "virtual" folders that can help you keep your data organized by giving you a single convenient place to manage and access files and folders stored in several different physical locations.

Why might this be useful? One example is if you have files on an external storage device—let's say a folder full of pictures on a USB flash drive. You could copy the pictures on this external device to the Pictures folder on your PC, but you might not necessarily want to do that. Perhaps your PC is low on storage space, or you may simply want to keep the pictures on the external device for reasons of portability.

In this scenario, to view and work with *all* of your pictures you'd have to continually jump between the Pictures folder and the external device in File Explorer, which can be cumbersome and time-consuming. But by adding the folder containing the pictures on the USB device to your Pictures Library, pictures from both locations (your PC and the external drive) are accessible from the same place in File Explorer.

Another example where using a Library might come in handy is when you're working on a project that consists of different kinds of files. For example, suppose that you're creating a presentation, proposal, or similar document that incorporates background music and/or images. Presumably the files that you'll use to create the document will reside in up to three different locations (i.e., the Documents, Music, and Pictures folders), which would make for a lot of back-and-forth while putting together the document.

You can create a new Library for the project, add all the folders you need for the project to that Library, and save yourself a lot of time and trouble when it comes to locating the files you want to work with.

---

It's important to note that when you add a folder to a Library (or remove one) you're not actually changing where any files or folders are stored, so no data is ever copied, moved, or deleted. Adding a folder to a Library simply provides a convenient shortcut to the folder from inside the Library regardless of where the folders are actually stored.

---

## WHICH FOLDERS ARE INCLUDED IN A LIBRARY BY DEFAULT?

That depends on your version of Windows and how you got it (i.e., whether it came with your PC or you upgraded to it from a previous version). Both Windows 8.1 and Windows 10 include default libraries for the four primary kinds of files—Documents, Music, Pictures, and Video—which always include the user's folder for that particular kind of file. So, for example, your Documents Library always includes your Documents folder, and your Pictures Library always includes your Pictures folder.

Libraries may also include the Public folder for a kind of file, and if you sign into Windows with a Microsoft account, your OneDrive folder for that kind of file as well. So the Documents Library on a Windows 8.1 PC that was upgraded from Windows 7 or 8 may include your Documents folder and the Public Documents folder, whereas if you buy a Windows 10 PC and sign in with a Microsoft account, your Pictures Library will include your Pictures folder and your OneDrive Pictures folder. (For more on OneDrive, see Chapter 8.)

An exception to this is the Videos Library, which does **not** automatically include the OneDrive Videos folder.

Regardless of which folders a library includes by default, you are free to add or remove folders in any library.

Incidentally, if one of Windows' built-in libraries is ever missing, you can usually bring it back by right clicking or long tapping Libraries in the Navigation pane and choosing Restore default libraries.

## Adding a Folder to a Library

To add a folder to an existing Library, right click or long tap it, select Include in library, then select the Library that you want to add the folder to, as shown in Figure 3-2. When you expand the Library in the navigation pane, you'll see that your folder has been added.

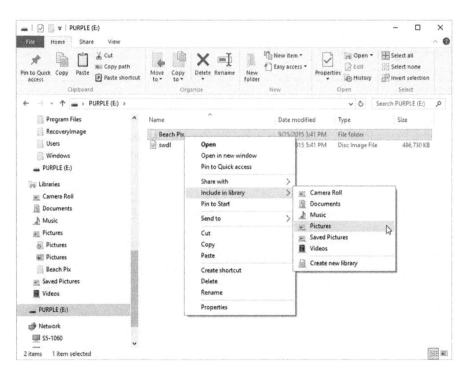

***Figure 3-2.*** *Adding a folder to an existing library. Notice that in this image the Pictures Library includes the user's PC and OneDrive Pictures folder as well as the newly added Beach Pix folder*

Notice that if you add a folder from an external storage device to a Library and then disconnect the device from your PC, it won't appear in the list of Library locations until you connect the device again.

## Creating a New Library

To add a folder to a new Library (i.e., a Library that doesn't exist yet), select the Create new library option as also shown in Figure 3-2. You'll see a new Library appear under the Libraries heading in the Navigation pane, as shown in Figure 3-3. Although the Library name will mimic the name of the folder that you used to create it (in this case Beach Pix), you're free to rename it to something more suitable.

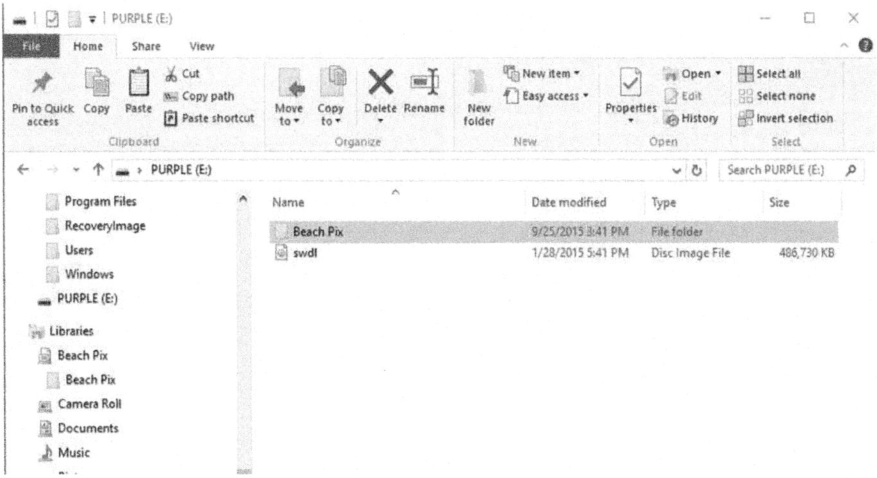

**Figure 3-3.** *Adding a folder to a new Library*

An alternate way to create a new Library is to right click or long tap Libraries in the Navigation pane, then choose New Library. The library will be called "New Library," which you can replace with the name of your choice.

---

A folder can be part of more than one Library.

---

# Removing a Folder from a Library

To remove a folder from a Library, find the Library in the navigation pane and expand it. Then right click or long tap the folder you want to remove and select Remove location from library (Figure 3-4).

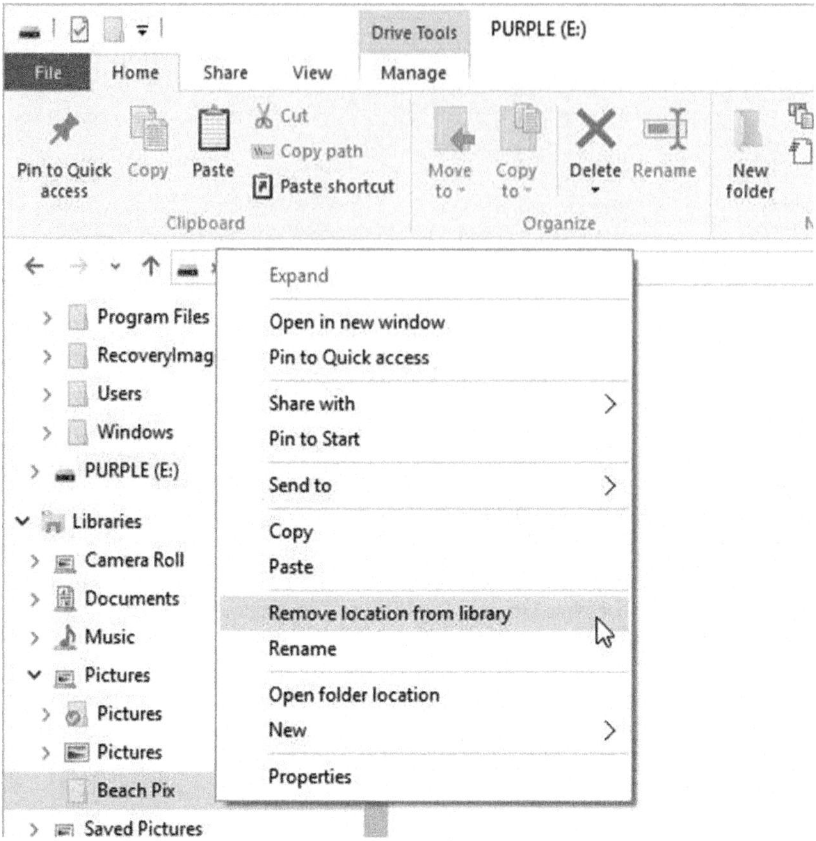

***Figure 3-4.*** *Removing a folder from a Library*

## Customizing Libraries

Windows allows you to customize certain aspects of a Library, including how it appears in File Explorer and where it saves files by default. To access these options, right click or long tap on a Library in the Navigation pane and select Properties to display the window shown in Figure 3-5.

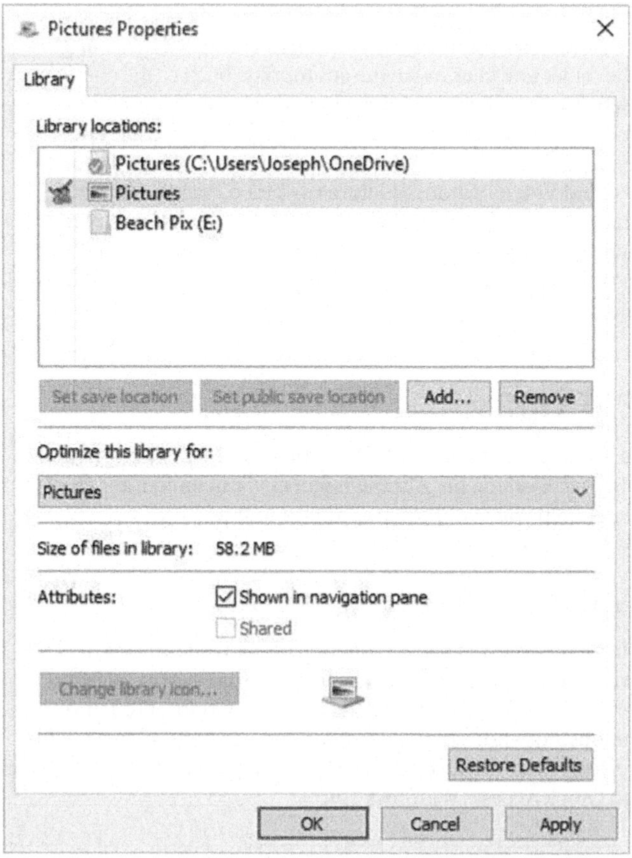

***Figure 3-5.*** *Customizing library options, including where files are saved and how they're displayed*

You'll see a list of folders that are part of the Library, and, beneath that, buttons labeled Set Save location and Set public save location. Recall that Libraries aren't physical storage locations, so these two buttons let you specify which folder an item will be stored in when you copy, move, or save it to the Library. The Set save location determines where you will save items in the Library, while Set public save location determines where those with whom you may share the Library (e.g., other users of the PC, or other PCs in a networked HomeGroup) will save their files in the Library.

For more on sharing, see Chapter 10.

In Figure 3-5, the user's Pictures folder is both the save location and the public save location, which is why both buttons are disabled when that folder is selected. To change either save location, select the folder and click or tap the appropriate button (the check mark and/or sharing icons in the left margin will move to the new folder to reflect the change).

The Optimize this Library for menu lets you specify how you want the contents of the library to be displayed by default, and the available options are General Items, Documents, Music, Pictures, and Videos. Choose Pictures or Video, and the Library contents will be shown using large icons, which is most suitable for those types of items. Similarly, choosing Documents or Music will display the Library contents in Details view, with column headings relevant to the specific kind of file—Music, for example, will display artist and album info.

# File Management Tips

A common challenge in file management is trying to find out what the heck happened to the file you were just looking at or working on. Although you may not encounter all of the following issues, these tips can help you avoid some common pitfalls.

## Finding Files Downloaded from the Internet

When you download a file from the Internet (e.g., a program) via a Web browser, it is typically saved to your Downloads folder no matter which Web Browser you're using (i.e., Microsoft Edge or Internet Explorer, Google Chrome, Mozilla Firefox, etc.). If your browser doesn't offer you an obvious shortcut to this folder, you can access it from File Explorer as shown in Figure 3-6, where it will appear under the This PC heading as well as Favorites (Windows 8.1) and Quick Access (Windows 10).

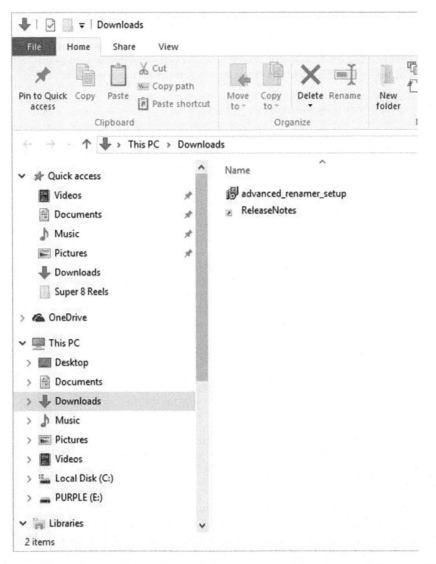

***Figure 3-6.*** *Files downloaded from the Internet are typically stored in the Downloads folder*

## Creating a New Copy of an Existing File

If you're like many people, you often create new documents by creating a copy of an existing file and then making changes to it. Although you can accomplish this by using File Explorer to make a copy of your original file and then renaming and modifying the copy, a better option is to use the Save As feature.

To do this, find the file that you want use as your starting point and open it. Then, before making any changes to the file, select Save As (typically found under the File menu) and type a new name over the existing one—which should be highlighted—and click or tap Save (Figure 3-7). You've now created a new version of the file with a new name and are free to modify it without changing anything about the original file.

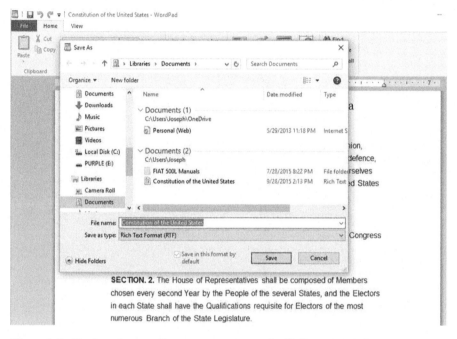

***Figure 3-7.*** *Use Save As to easily create a new copy of a file from an existing one*

# Opening a File from an Email

Here's a trap that many of us fall into. You receive an email with a file attached and open the file attachment from within the email to view, or even edit and save it. Later, you go looking for the file, but may not be able to find it anywhere except attached to the original email, and any changes you've made are nowhere to be found. You didn't imagine opening and/or saving the file, so where did it go?

When you open a file attachment directly from an email, you're typically opening a copy of the file that resides in an extensive set of temporary folders used to store items downloaded from the Internet (this includes images and graphics from webpages). A typical path to this folder will be something like C:\Users\Joseph\AppData\Local\ Microsoft\Windows\Temporary Internet Files\4MKZ395D, and because these folders are normally hidden from view in Windows, it can be quite difficult to find a file that you've inadvertantly saved into one of them.

To avoid this missing file syndrome, don't open file attachments directly from email. Instead, use your email's download option to download a copy of the attachment to a known location *before* you open it. (Depending on your email program, the download option may be a button or a link, or you may be able to right click or long tap the attachment and select Save As.)

---

If you opened an email file attachment in a program without remembering to save it first, the Save As feature will help you here as well, allowing you to save a new copy of the file to the location of your choice.

---

## Using AutoRecover/AutoSave

Many of us have had the experience of having a program crash and losing information as a result because the file that we were working on hadn't been recently saved.

The good news is that scenario isn't as common as it once was, in part because Windows has become much more reliable over the years, but also because of the AutoRecover/AutoSave feature that's included in almost all modern software.

For example, recent versions of Microsoft Office (which includes Word, Excel, and PowerPoint, among other programs) turns on AutoRecover by default and takes an automated snapshot of your open file every 10 minutes. In contrast, the free, open-source OpenOffice.org productivity suite saves its slightly differently named AutoRecovery info every 15 minutes.

Although these intervals are suitable for most people, they do mean that in rare circumstances a crash could wipe away as much as 10 or 15 minutes of work. If you'd like to shorten the AutoRecover interval in Microsoft Office, you can do so by selecting File, Options, Save, and adjusting the interval as shown in Figure 3-8. For OpenOffice, you'll find AutoRecovery settings under Tools, Options, Load/Save, General.

*Figure 3-8.* *Change Microsoft Office's AutoRecover interval to make save your open file information more frequently*

# CHAPTER 4

■ ■ ■

# Managing and Protecting Files with User Accounts

Consider this situation: someone in a household buys a new PC, and when setting it up for the first time, creates the obligatory Windows user account. That person then provides the password for the user account to other members of the household, who in turn use to log into the PC whenever they want to use it. This effectively means that multiple people are not only sharing a PC, they're sharing a single user account.

Although this scenario is all too common and may seem quite convenient, it's not recommended for a number of reasons, not the least of which is that it deprives each user of the ability to customize the look, feel, and behavior of the PC according to their own individual preferences. But when it comes to file management, sharing a user account is a particularly bad idea for two reasons.

First, it results in multiple people's files being comingled in the same set of user folders (e.g., Documents, Pictures, Videos, etc.) with no easy way to know which files belong to which person. It also means each user of the shared account is free to view, modify, or delete another person's files (inadvertently or otherwise)—after all, as far as Windows is concerned, there's only one person using the PC.

The other reason sharing a single account among multiple people is asking for trouble is because the first account created on a Windows PC is automatically made an Administrator account, an account type that has unrestricted access to the PC and its settings (as opposed to a Standard account, which has limited access).

This is important because when you're logged into Windows as an administrator, you're especially susceptible to malicious software (aka malware), which can more easily download and install itself onto the PC (sometimes in the background and without any overt signs that it's happened). And although many kinds of malware used to be content to be a nuisance (to hijack your browser or search engine, or to disable your PC), these days malware is much more likely to target your personal files for damage or destruction—even denying you access to your files unless you pay a ransom.

41

## BEWARE OF RANSOMWARE

Ransomware is a relatively new and particularly dangerious kind of malware that encrypts your files and demands that you buy the encryption key you'll need to regain access to them.

For more information on how ransomware works and how to protect yourself, see `https://blogs.sophos.com/2015/03/03/anatomy-of-a-ransomware-attack-cryptolocker-cryptowall-and-how-to-stay-safe-infographic/`.

When everyone using a PC logs in via an administrator account, the risk of a malware infection is much greater, and that's true even if you have antimalware software installed. The bottom line: to maximize the ability of users to organize and manage their own files, and minimize the risk of file damage or loss due to malware, each person using a PC should have their own nonadministrator account.

In this chapter, we'll outline the different types of Windows user accounts, show how to create an account for each user of a PC, and switch an account between the different types.

# Windows User Account Types

Windows (8.1) offers three different account types:

> Administrator—an Adminstrator account has full control over all aspects of the PC. It can install hardware or software, change security and other systemwide settings, create or make changes to other user accounts, and access files and folders belonging to other users.

> Standard—a Standard account can perform most everyday tasks on a PC but can only change settings that affect that specific account (things such as desktop background, etc). It can't install software or change settings that affect the entire PC or other user accounts, and it can't access files or folders belonging to other accounts.

> Guest—a Guest account, which is turned off by default, is a special account intended for temporary use by those who don't have a personal account on the PC (e.g., household guests). Someone using the Guest account can't change PC settings or access files or folders belonging to other user accounts.

When you set up the first account on a PC, it is automatically made an Administrator account (each Windows PC must have at least one administrator account). Any subsequent accounts that you create are automatically made standard accounts (although you can change them to administrator accounts afterward).

---

## MICROSOFT ACCOUNT VERSUS LOCAL ACCOUNT

When you create a new user account in Windows, you're given the choice to set it up as a Microsoft account or a Local account (although the process clearly steers you toward the former). This distinction is separate from the account types just discussed—for example, an administrator or standard account can be either Microsoft or Local.

There are several important differences between a Microsoft account and a Local account, but as far as file management is concerned, the most important difference is that when you log into a PC using a Microsoft account, it also automatically logs you into various Microsoft online services (including its OneDrive cloud storage).

---

# Creating New User Accounts

To set up a new user account (in Windows 8.1), search for "add user" and run *Add, delete, and manage other user accounts*. Then click or tap Add an account and you'll see the screen shown in Figure 4-1.

*Figure 4-1.* *From here you can create either a Microsoft or Local account*

If you already have a Microsoft account, enter the email address you use to sign into it in the space provided. The email address and password associated with the Microsoft account will also be used to log into the PC.

If you don't have a Microsoft account but want one, click or tap *Sign up for a new email address* and follow the steps to create a new account.

If you'd prefer to create a local account instead, click or tap *Sign in without a Microsoft account (not recommended)*, then click or tap Local account. You'll see the screen shown in Figure 4-2, where you can choose a username, password, and a password hint (which will be displayed if you ever forget your password).

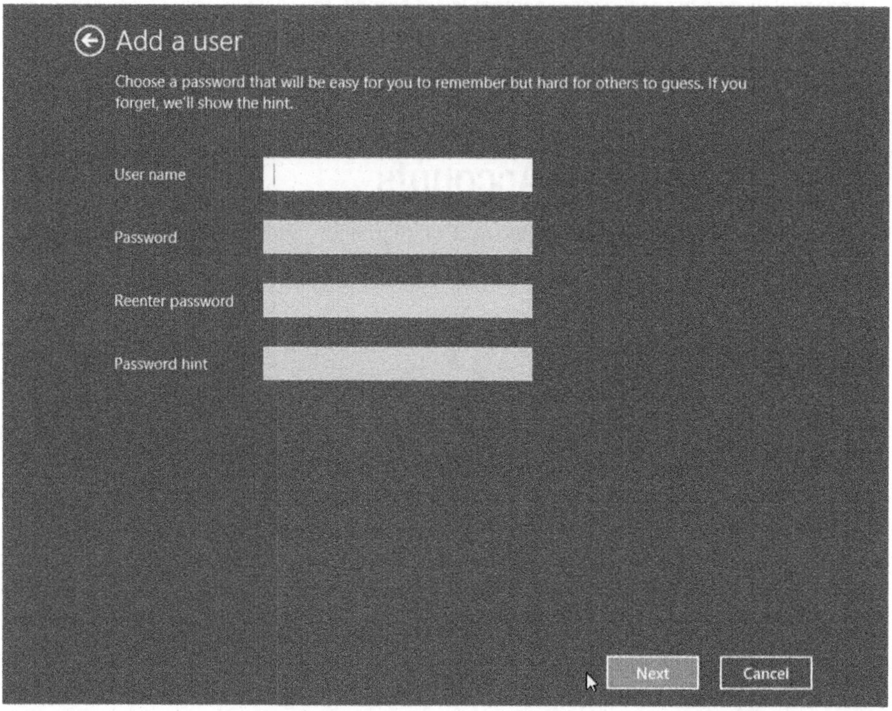

*Figure 4-2. Choose a username, password, and password hint to create a local account*

Windows will let you skip creating a password for local, nonadministrator accounts, but you should specify one anyway, if only to prevent people from inadvertently using an account that doesn't belong to them.

## WHY IS SKIPPING A MICROSOFT ACCOUNT NOT RECOMMENDED?

Mainly because using a local account means that you'll need to log into your Microsoft account separately when you need to access Microsoft services, such as downloading an app from the Windows Store, using Skype, or accessing files stored on OneDrive. Also, if you use a Microsoft account and log into another PC, some of your settings and preferences will follow you to that PC.

But if you're willing to forgo these conveniences, there's nothing harmful about using a local account to login to your PC.

## ADDING NEW USERS IN WINDOWS 10

Windows 10 supports almost all of the same account types as Windows 8.1 (except for the Guest account), but its process to add new users is slightly different. You can still start by searching for Add User, but in Windows 10 the setting you want to run is called **Add, edit, or remove other users**.

When you run it, you'll see the screen shown in Figure 4-3. To add an account for a family member with a Microsoft account, choose *Add a family member*. You'll be asked whether you want to set up the account for an adult or a child, and to provide an email address that's associated with a Microsoft account (or set up a new email address and Microsoft account).

45

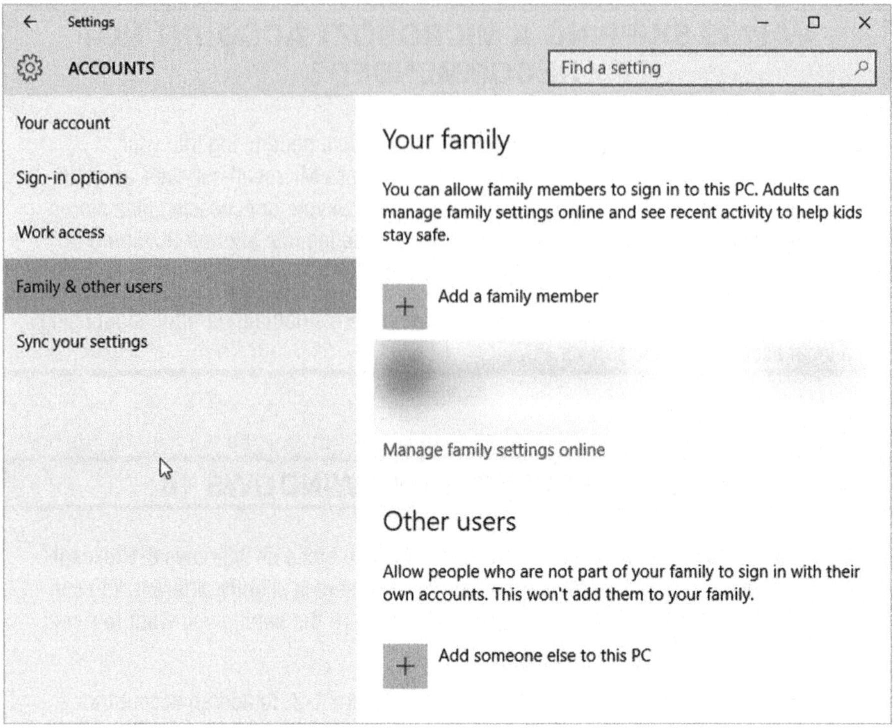

*Figure 4-3.* *Adding a user account in Windows 10 is slightly different than in Windows 8.1*

Setting up an account for a family member allows adults to monitor and manage kids' online activities.

To add an account for someone who is not a family member—and as there's no longer a Guest account in Windows 10 you may want to do this for a frequent visitor or houseguest—choose *Add someone else to this PC*. Then either enter their Microsoft account email address, or choose *The person I want to add doesn't have an email address* to create a Microsoft account for the user. Otherwise, choose *Add a user without a Microsoft account* to set up a local account. (Incidentally, this last option is how to create a local account for anyone, family member or not.)

# Turning on the Guest Account

As we mentioned previously, the Guest account is a special type of account available in Windows 8.1 (but not Windows 10). It's intended to give a visitor restricted access to your PC but doesn't allow the user to change any PC settings or access other users' files.

---

Note that the Guest account is always named "Guest" and can't have a password.

---

To enable the Guest account, search for "guest" and choose *Turn guest account on* or off to bring up the window shown in Figure 4-4. Click or tap on the Guest account, then click or tap the Turn on button.

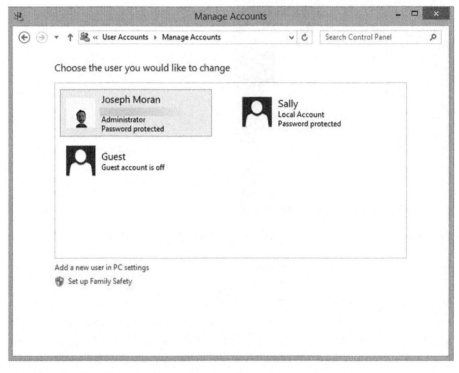

***Figure 4-4.*** *Select the Guest accout, then choose Turn on to activate it*

# Switching Between User Accounts

When you start up a PC that has more than one Windows account on it, all of the accounts are displayed on the login screen so that you can choose which account you want to use. But even if someone else has already logged into a PC with another account, you can still log in to that PC with your own account, and do so without disturbing anything the first person has in progress.

To log into a PC with a new account, click or tap on the user's name on the Start screen, then click or tap the new account you want to use (Figure 4-5). The new account will be logged in, and the existing account will be locked (but still be running in the background).

***Figure 4-5.*** *Click or tap on the currently logged-in user's name to log in with a new account*

---

Did you notice the Lock option in Figure 4-5? It's a good idea to select it when you're planning to leave a PC unattended for any length of time. This will keep your stuff open and/or running (files, apps, etc.) undisturbed and also ensure that no one else will be able to use your account. If, as in our example, you have multiple user accounts on your PC, when a PC's been locked you'll see a left-facing arrow next to the user'sname on screen (Figure 4-6). Click or tap the arrow to sign in with an additional account.

---

*Figure 4-6.* On a locked PC, tap or click the left-facing arrow to sign in with another account

To lock an account or switch between accounts from the Windows 10 desktop, click or tap the Windows logo at lower left, then click or tap the username, as shown in Figure 4-7.

*Figure 4-7.* Lock or switch accounts in Windows 10

## MULTIPLE ACCOUNTS AND PC PERFORMANCE

When multiple accounts are running on a PC simultaneously, each one consumes computing resources (i.e., processor power and RAM) even if it's not being actively used. On some PCs—particularly those designed to be small and lightweight rather than for high performance—running too many accounts at once may noticeably slow down the PC's responsiveness, but most should be able to accommodate two or perhaps three simultaneous accounts with minimal slowdown.

# Changing Between Account Types

Once an account has been set up as administrator or standard, Microsoft or local, it need not remain that way forever. Here's how to change between different account types.

## Standard ←→ Administrator

To change a Standard account to Administrator or vice versa, search for and choose user accounts to display the screen shown in Figure 4-8. To change the account you're currently using, choose *Change your account type*. To change a different account, first choose *Manage another account*, then select the account you want and choose *Change the account type*.

***Figure 4-8.*** *Change an account type from Administrator to Standard or vice versa*

Remember that the more administrator accounts there are on a PC, the greater the opportunity for problems as a result of malware. We recommend sticking to a single administrator account if at all possible.

## Microsoft ←→ Local

To switch from a Microsoft account to a local account or vice versa, first log in with the account you want to change, then search for and choose *Manage your account*. You'll see the screen shown Figure 4-9, and under your account name there will be a link labeled Disconnect (if your account is a Microsoft account) or Connect to a Microsoft account (if it's a local account). Just click or tap the link to switch to the other account type.

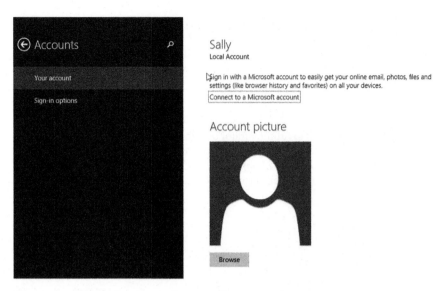

*Figure 4-9.* *Change an account from Local to Microsoft or vice versa*

In Windows 10, instead of Disconnect/Connect, the option provided is to *Sign in with a Microsoft account* (or local account) *instead.*

■ ■ ■

# CHAPTER 5

# Managing and Reclaiming Disk Space

Thanks to continuous advances in hard drive technology over time, those storage devices have gotten ever larger and cheaper—so much so that not that long ago the notion that the typical person might use up all of the storage capacity of a typical desktop or laptop PC seemed quite far-fetched.

These days, while it's still fairly unlikely that you'll fill your PC's storage entirely, it's not inconceivable either. There are a couple of main reasons for this, which we'll discuss in this chapter, along with how to check the amount of disk space in use (and thus how much is free). We'll also examine how to determine how your disk space is being used (apps, files, what kind of files, etc.), and will explore some ways to free up disk space if needed.

## Why Storage Space Can Run Low

This can happen for two main reasons, one of which is the type of files being stored. There once was a time when personal files consisted mostly of things such as documents and spreadsheets, and these file types that don't take up a particularly large amount of space. These days, people are much more apt to store things such as high-resolution photos and high-definition videos, and they, by contrast, consume an enormous amount of space.

Moreover, the proliferation of inexpensive digital cameras (and smartphones that are so equipped) allows almost anyone to generate a prodigious number of photos and videos over time (hundreds or thousands of files, or maybe even more). Chances are all of these photos and videos are finding their way to your PC, either because you manually transfer the files periodically, or because they are automatically transferred via a cloud storage/synchronization service.

The size of a given photo or video file depends on a number of variables, including the device used to take it and its image quality settings (as well as length, if it's a video). But here's a sense of how much space a photo or video can consume: a 16-megapixel photo—16 megapixels is a typical size for a photo taken by a high-end smartphone camera—takes up almost 5 MB of space, which means that roughly 200 photos consume about 1 GB, whereas RAW (i.e., uncompressed) photos from a digital SLR camera consume 10 times as much space. Similarly, 20 to 60 minutes of HD video can consume 4 GB.

The other reason that PC storage space might be in short supply is that your next PC (or even your current one) might actually have less storage than your last one did. This may at first seem counterintuitive, so let us explain.

As desktop PCs have declined in popularity compared to laptop PCs, and conventional large (sometimes known as full-sized) laptops lose favor to smaller, thinner, lighter alternatives, the amount of storage space a PC offers tends to decline. Whereas a desktop system might come with a hard drive several terabytes (TB) in size, most standard laptops generally offer somewhere between a half TB (500 GB) and 1 TB.

Especially thin and light models often provide even less storage, and many of the sveltest portable PCs, including many hybrid/convertible units (which function as either a laptop or a tablet), can sport as little as 32 or 64 GB of storage because they use SSDs rather than hard disks.

Unlike a conventional hard disk, which stores data on rotating magnetic platters, an SSD (Solid State Drive) stores data on memory chips. Although SSDs are much faster than hard disks, they are also considerably more expensive, and thus come in much smaller capacities.

# Checking Overall Disk Usage

Checking how much disk space is in use is a relative simple task in both Windows 8.1 and Windows 10. Just run File Explorer by pressing the Windows and E keys simultaneously or by clicking the yellow folder icon on the taskbar. Then from within File Explorer select *This PC* in the left pane. Now, under the **Devices and drives** heading in the right pane, look for the item labeled **(C:) (it may be labeled "Local Disk", "Windows", "OS", or something else** (Figure 5-1). This will show the size of your drive and how much space is left on it. (Note that Drive C: represents your PC's main hard drive; you may also see other drives listed if your PC has them.)

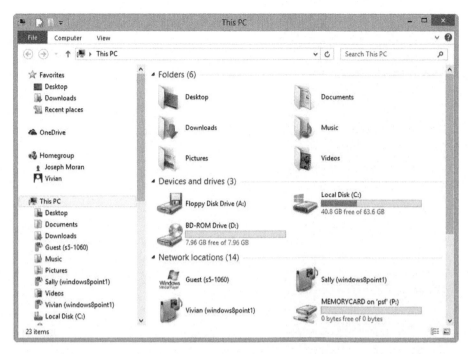

***Figure 5-1.*** *Use File Explorer to check how much disk space you have in total, and how much is left*

That horizontal "fuel gauge" bar lets you see at a glance roughly how much space you have left. When disk space approaches empty, the bar turns red.

# Determining What's Taking Up Space

It's one thing to know how much disk space you're using, but you get more insight by knowing exactly **how** that space is being used. To have a look at this in Windows 8.1, go to the Start screen and search for *disk space.* Then choose *Free up disk space on this PC.* This will display the screen shown in Figure 5-2. Up top you'll see the same overall disk usage info that we saw earlier from File Explorer. Below that, you'll see how much space is being used by Windows Store apps, various types of files, and deleted files that are still in the Recycle Bin.

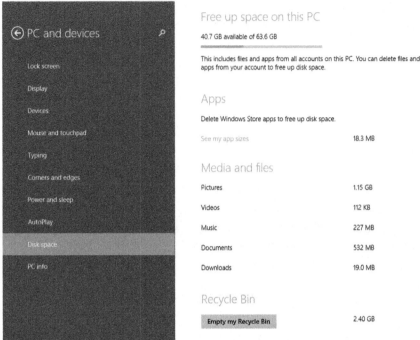

**Figure 5-2.** *Here you can see how much disk space is used by Windows Store apps and various types of files*

Note that the amount of disk space shown under Apps refers only to the kind that you download from the Windows Store. It doesn't include apps downloaded and/or installed from other sources (websites, discs, etc.). To see how much space those apps are taking up in Windows 8.1, right-click or long tap the Windows logo at lower left and choose Programs and Features. This works in Windows 10 as well, but the Apps category in Windows 10 lists space used by both kinds of apps. See the Windows 10 sidebar on the next page for more info on other changes.

---

# WINDOWS 10

To see how your disk space is being used in Windows 10, the process is a bit different. Search for **Settings** and then choose **System,** and, finally **Storage**. At the top of the screen shown in Figure 5-3 you'll see overall disk usage, although note that, unlike Windows 8.1, Windows 10 reports how much space is **used** instead of how much is **free**). For a detailed breakdown of how that space is used, click or tap on This PC (C:). Windows 10 displays a more comprehensive list of categories than Windows 8.1, and, unlike its predecessor, in Windows 10 you can click on a category for additional detail and options to free up some space.

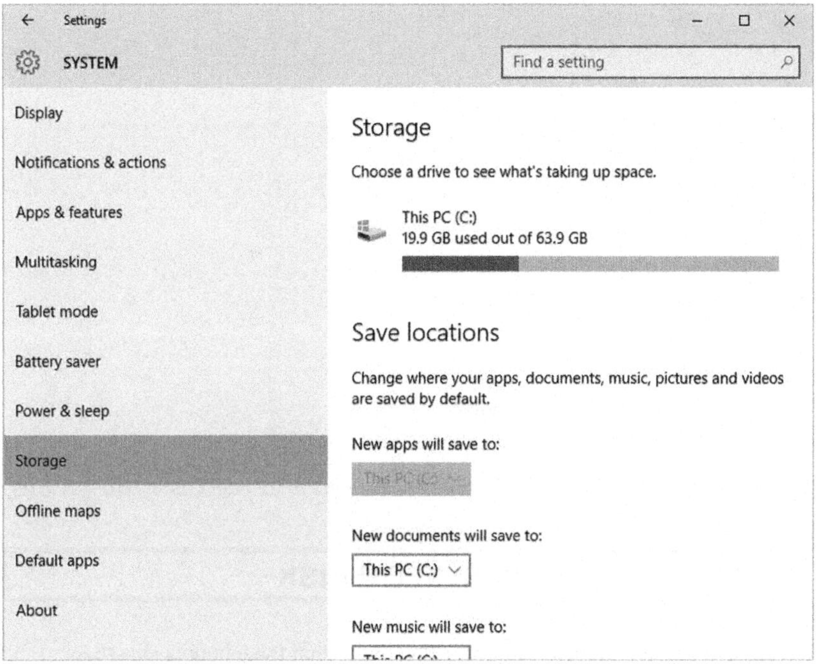

**Figure 5-3.** *Checking drive space usage in Windows 10.*

Here you may also modify the default Save locations of for various kinds of files (provided that your PC has more than one storage location available, of course).

Incidentally, to see how much space any particular folder in Windows (8.1 or 10) is using, first find it in File Explorer, then right click or long tap it, select Properties, and refer to Size, as shown in Figure 5-4.

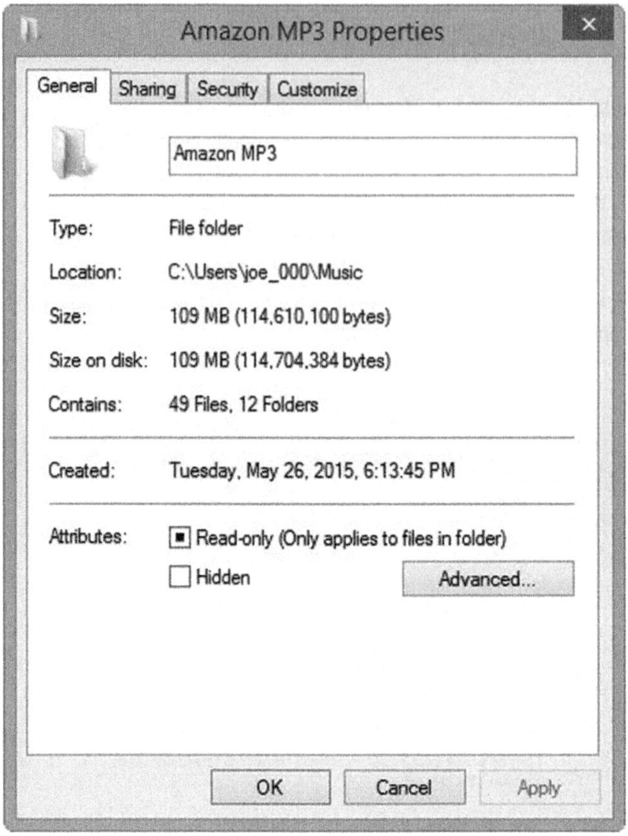

*Figure 5-4. View the Properties of any folder from File Explorer to see how much space it is using*

## SIZE VS. SIZE ON DISK

When viewing the size of a folder, you will often notice that the amounts shown for Size and Size on disk do not agree.

What gives? Disks are divided into many small chunks called blocks, and each block can store data from only one file (even if the file doesn't entirely fill up the block). Because most files won't fit perfectly into a given number of blocks, they almost always leave part of the last block empty, and although this space can't be used by another file, practically speaking it's still been used.

So in a nutshell, Size represents the actual size of your files, while Size on disk represents that plus the empty space those files consume. The upshot is that if you were to delete the folder, the Size on disk is the amount of space that would be reclaimed.

# Getting Even More Detailed Storage Info

If you want even more detailed information about storage usage than either Windows 8.1 or Windows 10 can provide, there are a couple of third-party tools that can do the job.

One particularly good (and free) option is WinDirStat (short for Windows Directory Statistics), which you can download at windirstat.info. Install WinDirStat on your system and let it analyze your hard drive (this can take a while) and you'll see a breakdown (Figure 5-5) that lists the size of every folder, lists various file types by color, and displays a corresponding map that helps you visualize how much of your storage each folder or file is consuming. You can even click on the map to jump to the item that area represents (or vice versa—click an item in the list and it's highlighted on the map). WinDirStat also lets you examine the contents of files, and, if desired, recycle or permanently delete them directly from the program.

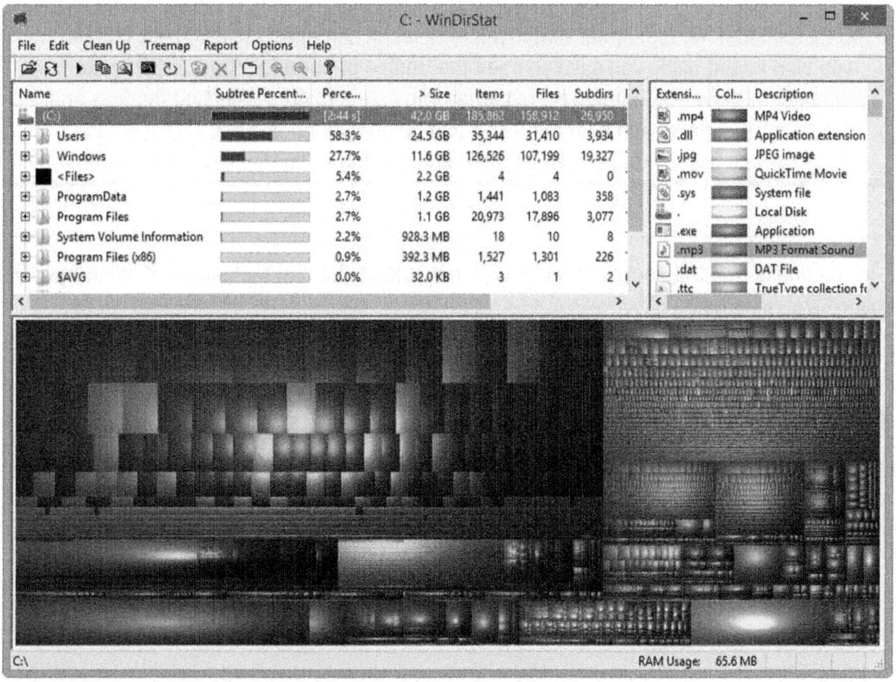

***Figure 5-5.*** *WinDirStat gives you a comprehensive look at everything on your hard drive*

An even more powerful option is TreeSize Personal. Although this program, which you can download at www.jam-software.com/treesize_personal/, isn't free, the cost is minimal ($25) and there is a 30-day free trial. TreeSize Personal has the same general features as WinDirStat but uses the familiar and arguably easier-to-use ribbon-style interface (à la Microsoft Office). TreeSize Personal also provides the ability to search for particular files of interest (e.g., biggest, oldest, or those that appear to be duplicates based on name, size, and date).

# How to Free Up Disk Space

## Empty the Recycle Bin

A quick and easy way to free up some disk space is to empty the Recyle Bin (i.e., permanently delete the files therein). In Windows 8.1, you can empty the Recycle Bin by clicking or tapping the button at the bottom right (see Figure 5-2).

In either Windows 8.1 or Windows 10, you can also empty it by right clicking or long tapping on the Recycle Bin icon and choosing Empty Recycle Bin.

This probably goes without saying, but we'll say it anyway—before emptying the Recycle Bin, review its contents to be sure there's nothing in there that you need.

---

## BYPASSING THE RECYCLE BIN

On a related note, remember that if you're deleting something that you are certain you won't want back, you save yourself the trouble of purging it from the Recycle Bin later and bypass the Recycle Bin when you delete it. After selecting the files and/ or folders, just press and hold the SHIFT key before you press or click Delete, and Windows will ask you to confirm whether you want to permanently delete the file.

---

Did you notice that the Recycle Bin is round in Windows 8.1 and rectangular in Windows 10? We have no idea why.

---

## Disk Cleanup

Another way to free up a bit of disk space in either Windows 8.1 or Windows 10 is via Disk Cleanup, a built-in utility that scans your hard drive for potentially unneeded files.

The easiest way to run Disk Cleanup in either operating system is via File Explorer. After selecting the drive, choose *Manage* then click or tap the Cleanup button (Figure 5-6).

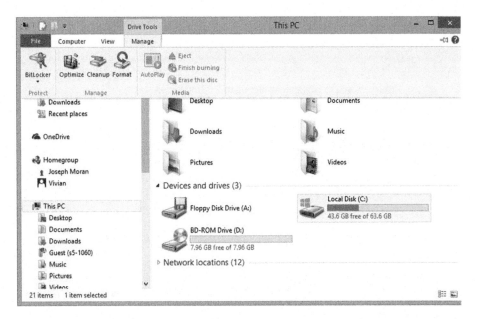

***Figure 5-6.*** *To run Disk Cleanup, first select the disk in File Explorer, choose Manage, and then Cleanup*

Once Disk Cleanup has examined your drive, it will display a window like the one shown in Figure 5-7 with a list of potential candidates for deletion. This will include, among other things, downloaded program files, temporary, log, and error files, and the contents of your Recycle Bin. Some of these items will automatically be selected by Windows, while others won't be.

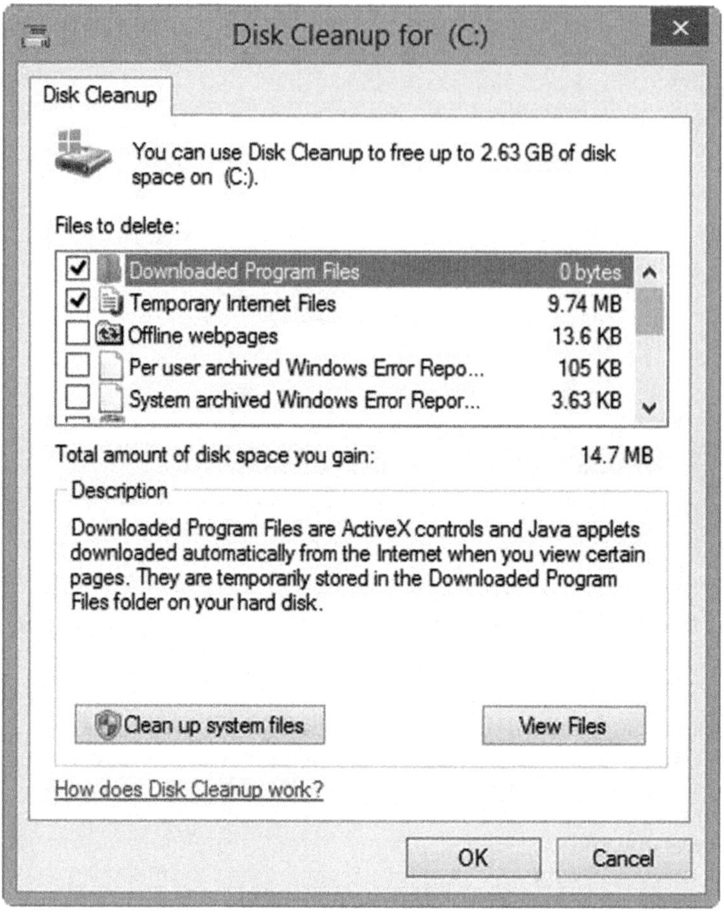

*Figure 5-7. Disk Cleanup scans for system files you can delete to free up space*

Just above the list, Disk Cleanup will tell you how much space you'd free up if all of the items were checked. Just below it, how much you gain based on the currently selected items is shown. Once you've made your selections and click OK, Windows will ask you to confirm that you want to permanently delete the files.

---

Not seeing much to delete in Disk Cleanup? Click the Clean Up System Files button (if you're an administrator) and Windows will rerun its scan, expanded to include things such as Windows Update files, which may let you reclaim considerably more space.

---

# CHAPTER 6

■ ■ ■

# Working with File Types and Programs (Apps)

One of the more frustrating aspects of using a PC is when you click or tap on a file to open it only to find that it doesn't open in the program you were expecting it to. This is especially irksome when a given file used to open in a familiar program but then suddenly and for no apparent reason opens in a different one.

In this chapter, we'll explore how Windows determines which program automatically opens your files and how to check in advance which program is configured to open which types of file. This is known as the *default program*. We'll also outline how to change the default program for a file type and then override that default for specific instances when you want to open a file in a different program than usual.

## PROGRAMS VS. APPS

Before we get started, let's talk about the difference between a "program" and an "app". Strictly speaking, there isn't any—both are a piece of software that you use to open a file, although the latter term is more often used to refer to programs downloaded from Microsoft's Windows Store (and which have a modern, touch-oriented interface). Microsoft uses both of these terms in Windows, and not entirely consistently, either. For the sake of clarity, we're going to refer mainly to "programs" in this chapter, but be aware that the terms are essentially synonymous.

## File Extensions

So how does Windows decide to automatically open file *x* using program *y*? Put simply, it looks at the type of file that you're opening—which is denoted by a three- or- four character suffix called an extension—and then starts up the program that's been defined as the default program for that file type.

Table 6-1 lists some frequently encountered file extensions and types.

***Table 6-1.*** *Common file extensions and types*

| Extension | Type | Extension | Type |
|---|---|---|---|
| .docx | Microsoft Word Document | .gif | Graphical Interchange Format image |
| .xlsx | Microsoft Excel Spreadsheet | .jpg | JPEG image |
| .pptx | Microsoft PowerPoint Presentation | .mp3 | MP3 audio |
| .pdf | Adobe Portable Document Format | .mp4 | MPEG-4 video |
| .txt | Plain text document | .mov | Apple QuickTime movie |

For a more comprehensive list of extensions and the file types that they represent, see `fileinfo.com/filetypes/common`.

Under normal circumstances, file extensions are hidden from view in File Explorer, but it's easy to make them visible. Click or tap the View menu and check the box labeled File name extensions (Figure 6-1); you'll see each file's extension displayed to the immediate right of its name. Checking this box makes file extensions visible not just in File Explorer but also in any other area where you view file listings, such as on the Desktop or when opening/saving files within programs.

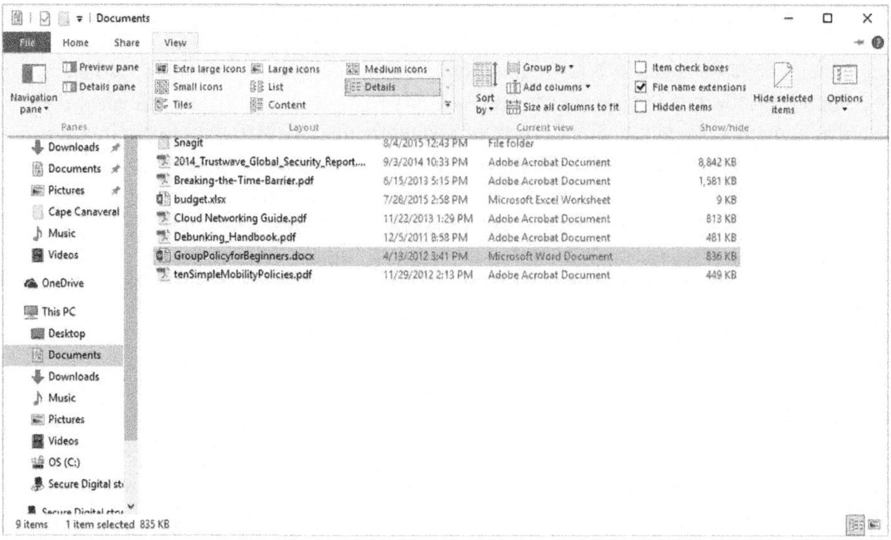

***Figure 6-1.*** *Making file extensions visible in File Explorer*

# File Associations

As a rule, you won't typically need to make file extensions visible because File Explorer's "Type" column and/or the file's icon will normally indicate what type of file you're dealing with. But, visible or not, file extensions are still important because they are what allows Windows to define a relationship between a particular type of file and the program (or programs) that can open that file.

This relationship is known as a file *association,* and the most important file association in Windows is the aforementioned default program, because it determines which program will automatically open a file when you click or tap on it.

Default programs can sometimes change unexpectedly, however. Often when you install a new program—or update an existing one—that's capable of opening a particular type of file, the program configures itself to automatically open *every* file type it knows how to handle. As it happens, most programs do give you the opportunity to review and override these changes during the install process, but they're often accepted without close scrutiny because of haste or inattention. This is typically how default programs get changed without anyone necessarily realizing that it has happened.

Fortunately, Windows lets you configure default programs and file associations so that you can always open the type of file you want with the specific program you want.

# Configuring Default Programs

To view and configure default programs in either Windows 8.1 or Windows 10, search for and select "Default Programs" (Figure 6-2), then choose the option labeled "Set your default programs".

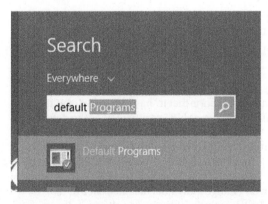

***Figure 6-2.*** *To configure default programs, start by searching for that term*

After a few seconds of load time, you'll see the window shown in Figure 6-3, listing all of your installed programs along the left pane. When you highlight a program in this left pane, you'll see configuration information about it in the right pane, including the name of the program, which company makes it, and, in some cases, a brief description of what the program does.

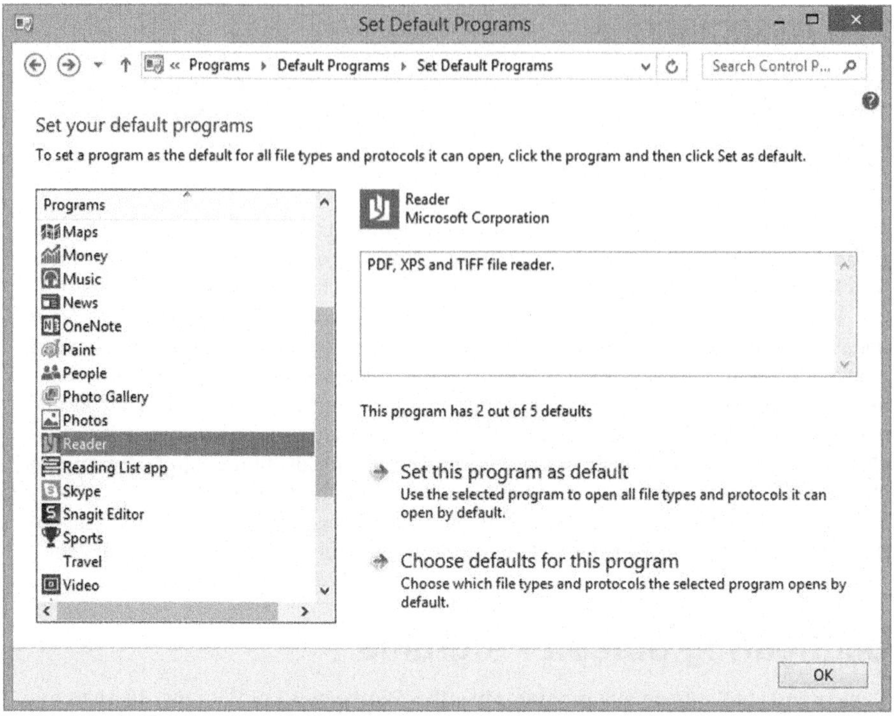

*Figure 6-3.* *Highlight a program on the left to view its configuration information on the right*

---

Your programs should be listed in alphabetical order, but you can switch to reverse alphabetical order by clicking or tapping the heading labeled "Programs".

---

Beneath this information, a line reports how many defaults the program is configured for. In other words, a program that reports that it "has 2 out of 5 defaults" means that it is associated with five different file types but is configured as the default program for only two of them.

To make the highlighted program the default for all of its associated file types, just click or tap "Set this program as default" and you'll see the aforementioned line change to "This program has all its defaults".

Conversely, to view and/or selectively change individual defaults, click or tap "Choose defaults for this program" to display a window like the one shown in Figure 6-4. Then check the additional file extensions that you want the program to be the default for and click or tap Save.

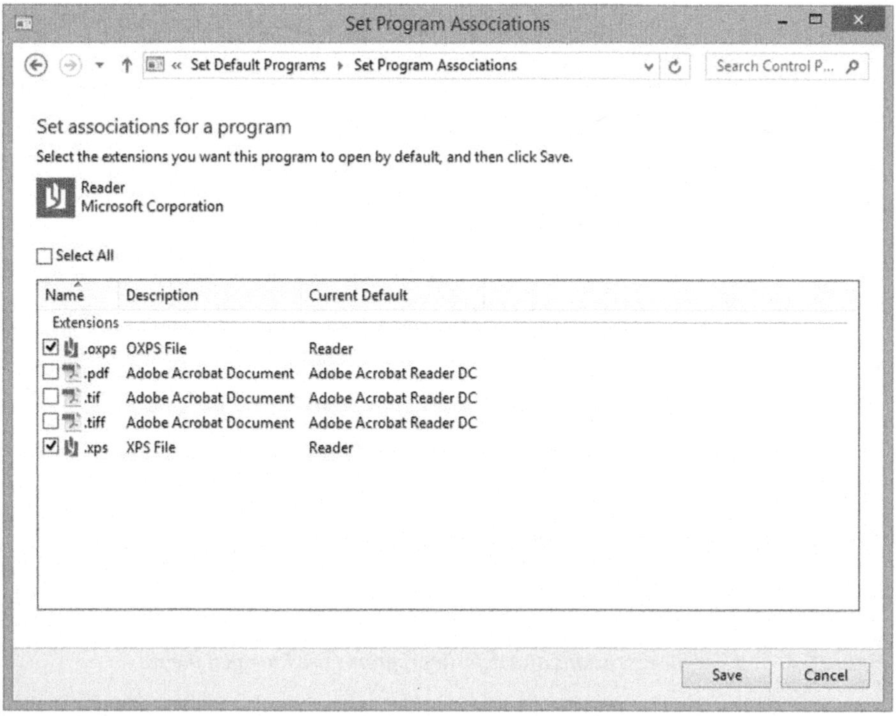

***Figure 6-4.*** *Check an extension and click Save to make the selected program the default for that file type*

Notice that if a file extension is already checked as shown in Figure 6-4, you can't uncheck it because that would eliminate the file's default program without specifying a new one. To change the default program for a specific file extension, see the next section.

# Configuring Default Programs by File Extension

The process that was just outlined is intended for situations in which you have a favorite program and want it to be the default for every file that it can open, or when you want a particular program to open specific additional file types that does not currently open. Put another way, once you've specified the program, you can specify the file extensions that it will automatically open.

If, by contrast, you approach the situation from the opposite perspective—you have a particular file type in mind and you want to choose a view or change the default program for it—the process is slightly different.

You still begin by searching for and running "default programs" as shown in Figure 6-2, but then you choose "Associate a file type or protocol with a program" to display the window shown in Figure 6-5, which lists file extensions, descriptions, and the current default program for each.

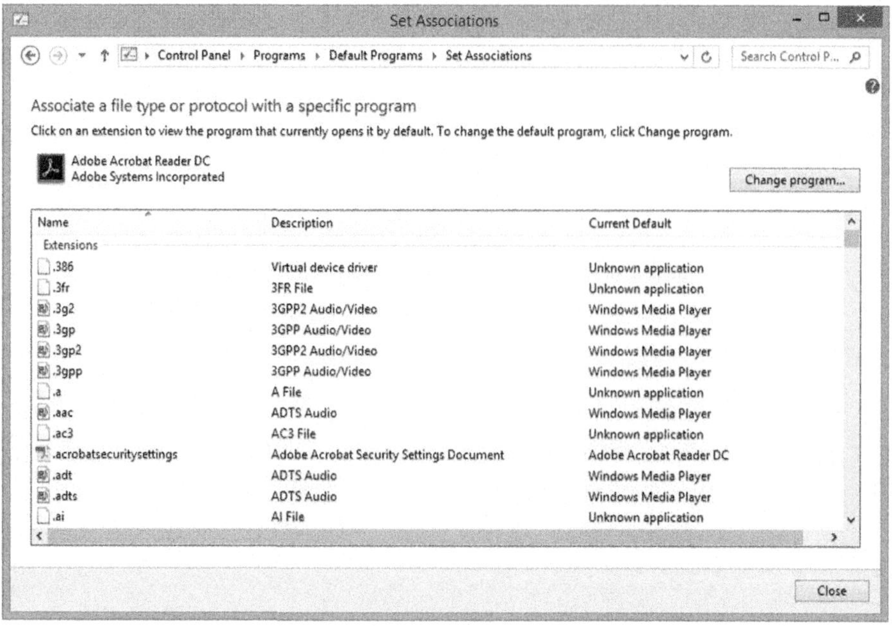

*Figure 6-5.* *A list of file extensions and default programs used to open them*

You'll find the list of file extensions arranged alphabetically just like the program list, but the file extension list is considerably longer as it will contain dozens if not hundreds of obscure or unfamiliar file extensions.

Also, be aware that a separate alphabetized list of protocols (which governs how Windows handles different kinds of Internet links in a Web browser or in certain programs) follows the file extension list, so that's what you'll be looking at if you scroll all the way to the bottom.

To change the default program for a given file extension, highlight it and click or tap the Change program button. Doing this with the .pdf file extension gives us the option to change the default program from Adobe Acrobat Reader DC to Microsoft's PDF Reader, which is built into Windows 8.1 (Figure 6-6).

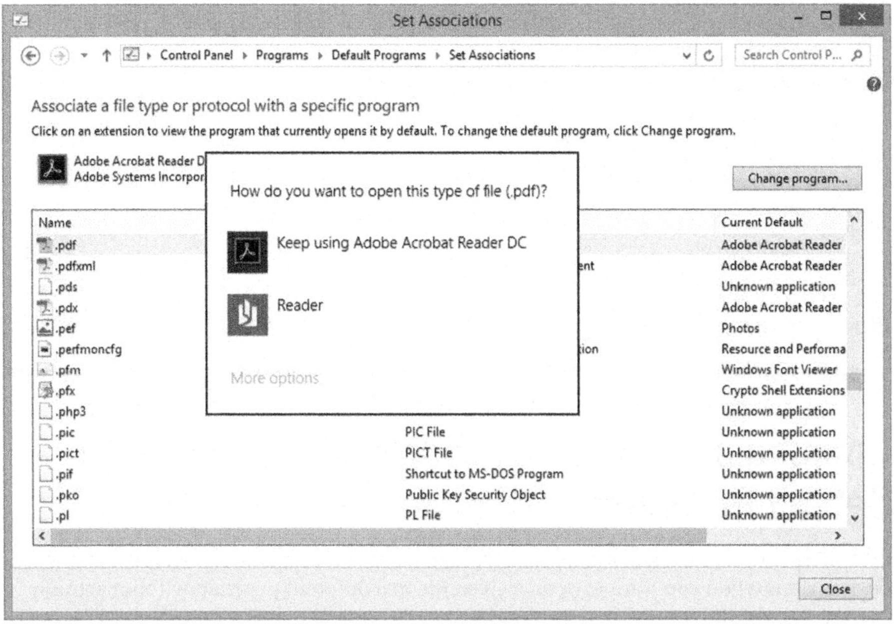

*Figure 6-6. Changing the default program for PDF files*

(Notice that the options presented will vary depending on which file extension you select, which programs you have installed, and even which version of Windows you are using.)

Selecting More options, as shown in Figure 6-6 (called More apps in Windows 10), will display additional program choices for opening the file, but those extra choices won't necessarily all be appropriate for the file. For example, for a .docx file (Microsoft Word Document), More options/apps will give you the option to open it in Microsoft Paint, an image editor, or Windows Media (audio/video) Player, neither of which were designed to open Micosoft Word documents. Suffice it to say that, as a rule, it's best to stick to the programs initially offered and avoid More options/apps unless you have a specific reason to choosing a different program.

## HOW DO YOU WANT TO OPEN THIS TYPE OF FILE?

Sometimes when opening a file you will see a popup window in the upper right corner of the screen, similar to the one shown in Figure 6-7, which is Windows proactively asking if you want to change the default program for that file type. This typically happens the first time that you try to open a particular file type on a PC, or after installing a new program that can open that file type (which gives you additional choices for a default program).

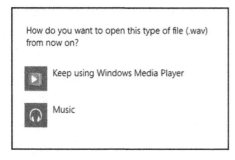

How do you want to open this type of file (.wav) from now on?

Keep using Windows Media Player

Music

*Figure 6-7. Windows will sometimes ask you to choose a default program for a particular file type*

# Opening a File with a Program Other than the Default Program

Even after you've chosen a preferred default program for a particular file type, there may be occasions when you want to open a given file in a different program without actually changing that default program. For example, you'll typically open video files in a player program, but if you want to edit a video you'll want to open it in an editing program instead.

Fortunately, Windows makes it easy to choose the program that you want to use each time you open a file. Just right click or long tap the file and choose "Open with" to display a list of appropriate programs (Figure 6-8). Select the program that you want and the file will open in that program without changing the default program.

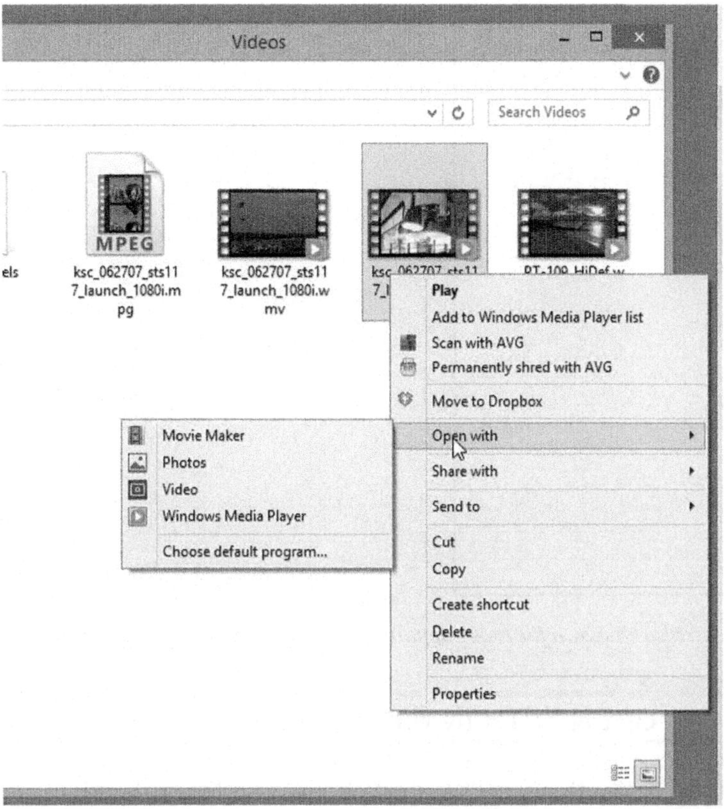

***Figure 6-8.*** *Open with lets you open a file using a program other than the default*

The Choose default program option in Figure 6-8 offers an alternative method to "Choosing default programs by file extension" described earlier. Select this item and you'll see a window like the one shown in Figure 6-9, allowing you to specify a new default app. Notice the check mark next to "Use this app for all...".

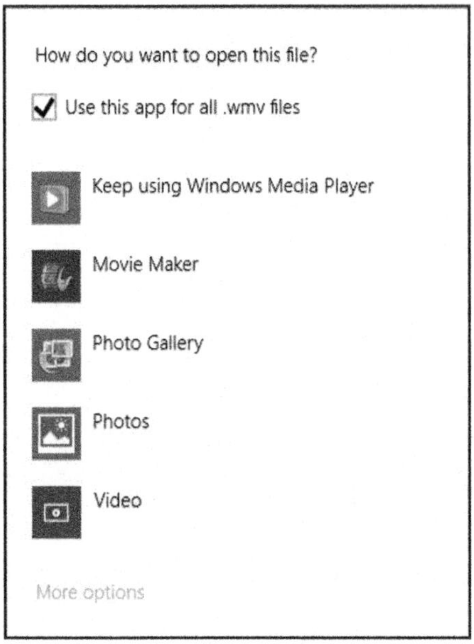

How do you want to open this file?

☑ Use this app for all .wmv files

▶ Keep using Windows Media Player

Movie Maker

Photo Gallery

Photos

Video

More options

*Figure 6-9.* *You can also change a file type's default program via the Open with menu*

## OPEN WITH IN WINDOWS 10

In Windows 10, the Open with menu's Choose default program option has been changed to Choose another app. You can still change the default program from here, but you must be sure to check the box labeled "Always use this app to open…" (Figure 6-10).

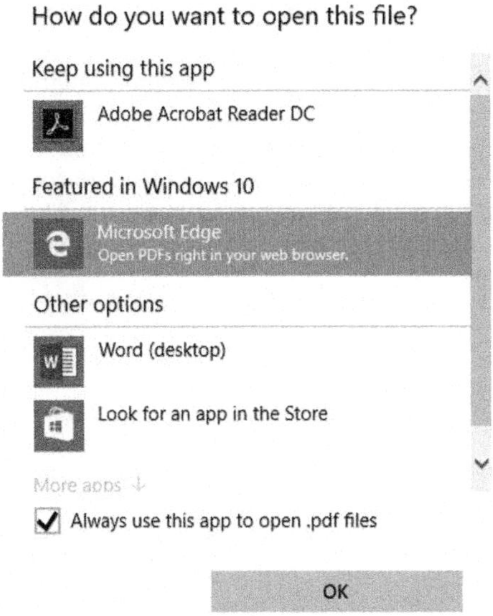

How do you want to open this file?

Keep using this app

Adobe Acrobat Reader DC

Featured in Windows 10

Microsoft Edge
Open PDFs right in your web browser.

Other options

Word (desktop)

Look for an app in the Store

More apps ↓

☑ Always use this app to open .pdf files

OK

***Figure 6-10.*** *Check "Always use this app..." to change the default program from the Open with menu in Windows 10*

# Opening a File When You Don't Have the Right Program

If you try to open a file for which you don't have the correct program, you'll see the window shown in Figure 6-11. This allows you to look for the right program in the Windows Store.

How do you want to open this type of file (.mpp)?

Look for an app in the Store

More options

***Figure 6-11.*** *What happens when Windows doesn't have a program capable of opening a file*

For example, in Figure 6-10, we're attempting to open a file with an .mpp extension, which was created in Microsoft Project and which we don't have installed on our PC. You could use the Look for an app in the Store option to find one, but another—and arguably better—option is to do an online search for the file extension or file type to find a program that will be able to open it.

Doing your own search is preferable because the Windows Store only has a limited number of programs/apps available, all of which use a modern, touchcentric interface (which you may or may not want). In addition, you need a Microsoft account to download anything from the Windows Store. In contrast, you'll almost always have more and better options when you search for a program yourself.

# CHAPTER 7

■ ■ ■

# Searching for Files

Even if you're fairly conscientious about how you store and organize your files, there will often be times when you need a particular document, picture, and so on, and you aren't quite sure exactly where to find it.

To help you find your file, Windows' built-in search feature makes it easy to do a quick search of all of the locations on a PC where a user's personal data is typically stored. You can also use File Explorer to perform a more targeted search of specific folders and/or search based on various file attributes such as the kind of file, its size, or when it was last modified.

## Windows 8.1 Quick Search

The easiest way to do a quick file search in Windows 8.1 is to press the Windows logo key + F and enter your search keyword—typically, this will be the filename, or as much of it as you know. Windows will display a partial list of results (Figure 7-1), so if you see the file you're looking for in the list, just click or tap to open it.

***Figure 7-1.*** *From anywhere in Windows 8.1, use the Windows logo key + F to perform a quick file search*

If you don't see the file that you want, click or tap the magnifying glass icon to the right of the search box and you'll be able to view the complete search results, which will be divided into three categories (if applicable)—documents, songs, and photos or videos (Figure 7-2).

*Figure 7-2. Click or tap the magnifying glass to the right of the search box to summon the complete list of results*

Your search results will typically include files with names that don't necessarily match your keyword, because in the case of documents (e.g., Microsoft Word, Microsoft Excel, Adobe PDF), Windows matches your keyword against a file's contents as well as its name (which is very handy when you don't necessarily know the name of the file you want, but do know to what it pertains). For example, searching for "tax" might produce a match to a file explicitly named "tax return," but it also might result in matches to additional files named "budget" or "form1040" if the data in those files includes the word "tax."

# Windows 8.1 File Explorer Search

Doing a quick search for a file as just described is easy, convenient, and will very often lead you to what you're looking for. However, because searching this way only allows you to search based on a keyword and can only search *all* indexed locations (as opposed to specific locations), you may also have to wade through a high number of matches to find a specific file.

For much greater control over how and where you search, use File Explorer. When you're in Windows 8.1's desktop mode, you can reach File Explorer by clicking or tapping its icon in the taskbar. Otherwise, right click or long tap the Windows logo icon at the lower left and select File Explorer.

---

You'll see a Search option right under File Explorer in the aforementioned Windows logo menu. This does an expansive "Everywhere" search for apps, files, settings, as well as an Internet search of whatever term you type in. Although this search mode is handy for general searches (other ways to invoke it are Windows key + S or simply typing a search term from the Start screen), it is best to avoid it when you're only looking for files.

---

Every File Explorer window contains a search box near the upper right, and inside this box you'll see text indicating where the search will be focused based on your location (Figure 7-3). For example, if you have This PC selected in File Explorer, the search box will display Search This PC; if you have the Documents folder selected, the box will display Search Documents, and so forth. Moreover, as you go deeper into a series of subfolders, the search box will always update to reflect the folder currently being viewed.

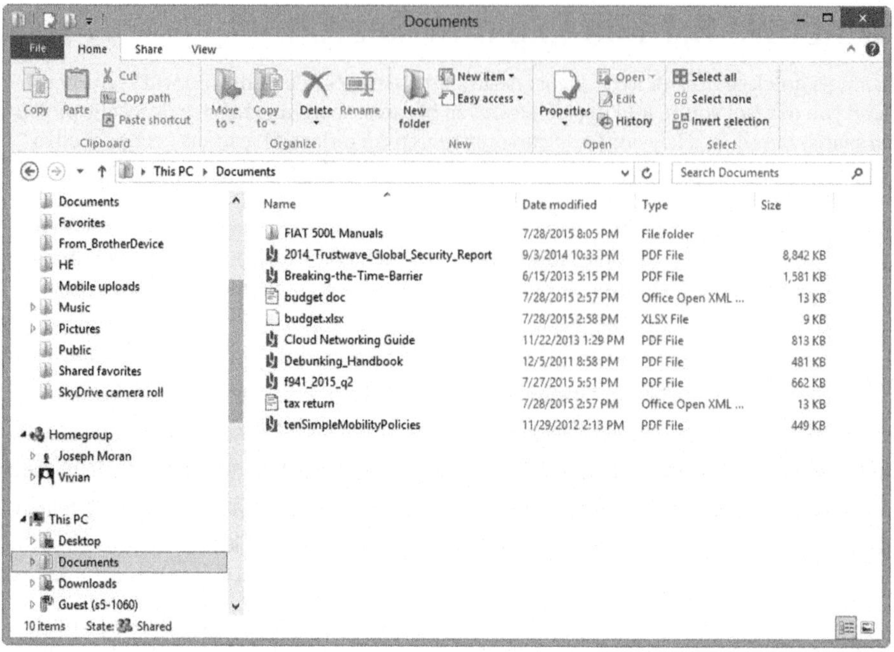

**Figure 7-3.** *The labeling of File Explorer's search box will always reflect the location that you've selected*

When you start typing your search term into the box, you'll immediately see the results appear below. As you continue typing, the search results will continually update to reflect what you've typed. You will also likely notice your search term highlighted in file listings when they match the name or contents of Microsoft office files (Figure 7-4).

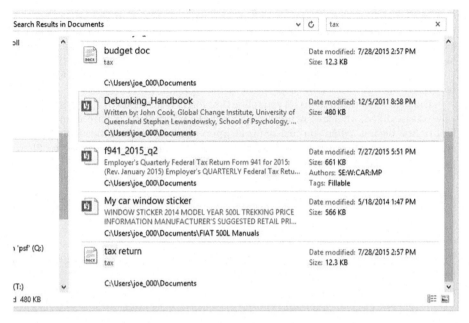

***Figure 7-4.*** *In most cases, your search term will be highlighted in results indicating whether it appears in a file's name, contents, or both*

---

Notice that for PDF files you'll only see your search term highlighted if it appears in the file's title or metadata. (Metadata is information about a file that is contained within its properties. For example, metadata about a document might include the title, subject, or author.)

---

## Search Tools

You'll probably notice that as soon as you click or tap inside File Explorer's search box, the menu items displayed at the top of the window switch to a set of Search Tools that allow you to customize your search location and apply various filters (Figure 7-5).

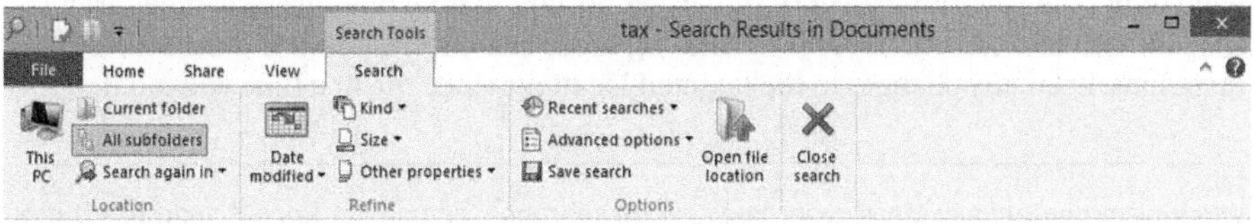

***Figure 7-5.*** *File Explorer's search tools*

From the leftmost set of menu items you can change the location of your search. By default, Windows automatically searches the folder you specify and all its subfolders (i.e., all folders contained within the one you're searching); therefore, you'll see "All subfolders" highlighted. Once you've entered your search term, click or tap the appropriate option to limit the search to the current folder or expand it to the entire PC. You can also refocus your search in a different location by choosing the Search again in option.

The next set of menu items let you refine (i.e., filter) your search by specifying when a file was modified, what kind of file it is (for example, a document, picture, or music file), or how big it is. When you click or tap an option and choose from the menu that appears (Figure 7-6), your search results will update accordingly. You'll also see the filter parameters added to the search box.

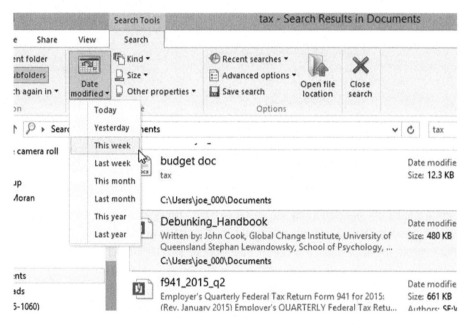

***Figure 7-6.*** *Use Search Tools to refocus or filter your search*

From the last set of menu items you can save your search, which is handy if you plan to do to the same search regularly. Saved searches appear in File Explorer's left pane under the Favorites category, and it's important to note that saved searches aren't snapshots in time. In other words, rerunning saved searches will return different results if there have been any changes to the targeted locations since the first time you ran it.

---

Windows automatically stores your last several searches, so use the Recent searches button to rerun past searches even if you didn't save them (or clear your search history instead).

---

# Advanced Query Syntax Searching

An even more powerful and focused way to search for files is by using Windows Advanced Query Syntax (AQS), a way to type file attribute filters directly into File Explorer's search box following your search term.

Let's say you wanted to search for files based on a term but wanted to limit your results only to files changed within a certain timeframe, as illustrated in Figure 7-6. To conduct this same search using AQS, you could type *<your search term> modified:* into the search box. As soon as you type the colon, a menu appears displaying the same timeframe options found in the previous figure, but with AQS you can also choose a specific date from the calendar or a custom range—just hold down Shift while clicking or tapping your beginning and ending dates (Figure 7-7).

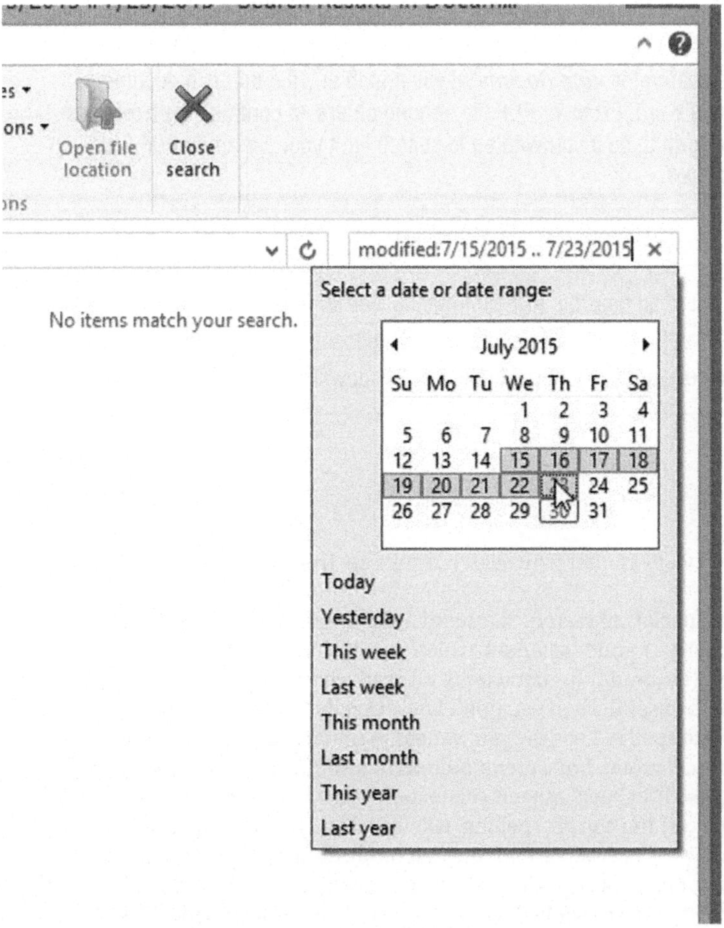

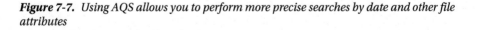

***Figure 7-7.*** *Using AQS allows you to perform more precise searches by date and other file attributes*

You can perform AQS searches using any of the options found within the Date modified, Kind, Size, or Other properties menus of Search Tools. (Note: choices available under Other properties will vary depending on the type of folder you're searching—for example, it will include "author" for Documents, "artist" for Music, and "date taken" for Pictures.)

It's worth noting that when searching via AQS you have the option to type past the menus if desired. In other words, type *kind:* and the relevant menu will appear, but you can ignore the menu and continue typing *kind:document* to complete your search.

## KIND VS. TYPE

I want to take moment to draw a distinction between the *kind* attribute and the *type* attribute, the latter of which is found in the Other properties menu.

Simply put, *Kind* is an umbrella term that refers to a certain category of file. For example, a file search for *kind:document* will match any file that is a document, which might be a Word, Excel, or PDF file, among others. In contrast, *type* refers to a particular file format, so if you wanted to search limit your search to PDF files, you would use *type:pdf.*

For an exhaustive list of all possible AQS commands, see `msdn.microsoft.com/en-us/library/aa965711(v=vs.85).aspx` (although the document is quite old, the AQS commands are still relevant to modern versions of Windows).

## Wildcards

Two other powerful ways to filter your search results are by using wildcards and/or Boolean operators.

Wildcards are special characters that stand in for other characters. Windows supports two wildcards: ? and * (asterisk), which stand in for a single character and a string of characters (i.e., multiple characters), respectively.

Wildcards can be useful when you don't know exactly what you're looking for, or may not know how to spell it. Let's say you wanted to search through your music for songs by a particular musical group, but weren't quite sure whether it was spelled "beatles" or "beetles". If you used "be?tles" as your search term, you'd be sure to find the songs regardless of which was the correct spelling, whereas if you based your search on the wrong spelling, you wouldn't (at least not the first time). Similarly, because the asterisk wildcard stands in for multiple characters, another way to find your beatles songs without having to know whether it was spelled "ea" or "ee" would be to search for "b*tles".

# Boolean Operators

Boolean operators allow for more powerful searches by letting you combine different keywords in order to include certain results or exclude others. Common Boolean operators include:

NOT (or -) finds items that contains one keyword but not the other. For example, Kansas NOT City would return files related to the state of Kansas, not the city of Kansas City (technically *cities*, as there's one in both Kansas and Missouri).

OR: Finds items that contain either keyword. For example, Kansas OR city would include results that contain "Kansas" or "City" but exclude those that include "Kansas City".

Quotation marks: Matches the exact phrase used to search, so searching for "tax" would exclude other results that also contained those letters (e.g., files about taxidermy).

Parentheses: Finds items that contain either word in any order. Example: (social networking) would also return results that include "networking social".

---

Boolean operators should always be typed in CAPTIAL LETTERS so that Windows can distinguish them from keywords.

---

# Understanding the Index

When you search for files in any of the standard Windows user folders—for example, Documents, Music, and Pictures—you'll see results very quickly if not nearly instantaneously. That's because Windows automatically indexes these standard storage locations (among others), which means that it analyzes them (and continually reanalyzes them in the background) so that it knows their contents in advance and thus can return results extremely quickly.

But if you were to do a search of certain other locations, such as "This PC" or an entire hard disk (e.g., Local Disk: C), you would find the results very slow in coming. That's because these searches contain areas that are not indexed; thus, Windows must actually search through them once you've specified what you're looking for. (Moreover, Windows doesn't search through file contents in nonindexed locations.)

To speed up searches in a nonindexed folder, add it to the index. From the Search Tools menu, click or tap Advanced options, select Change indexed locations, then select Modify and browse to the folder you want to add to the index (Figure 7-8).

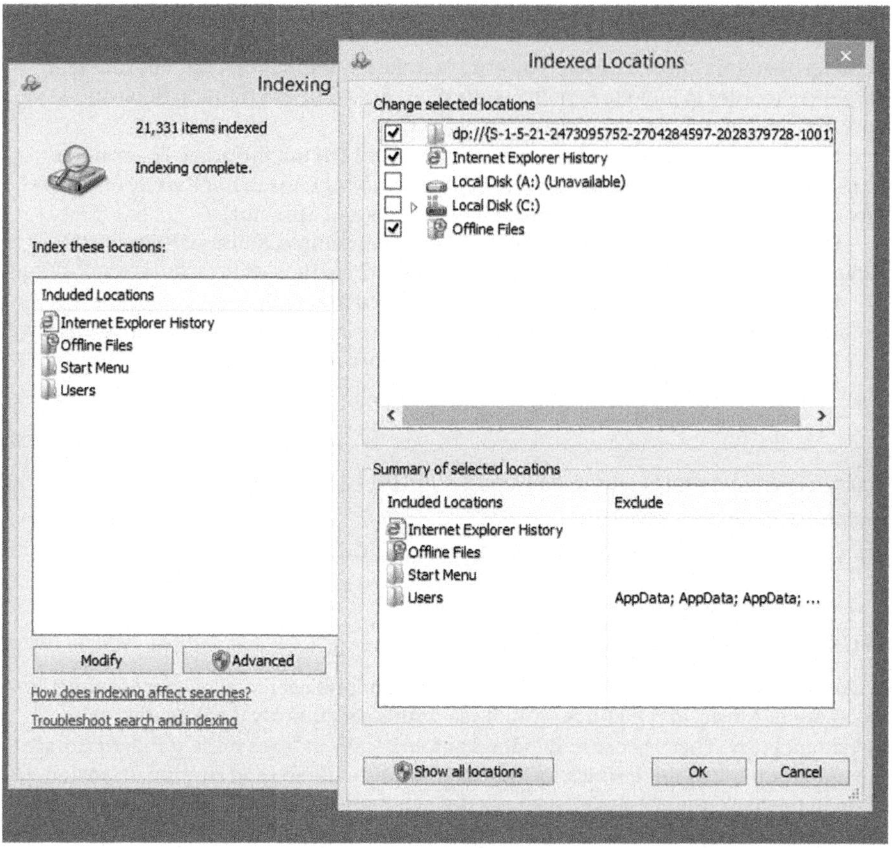

**Figure 7-8.** *Add folders to the index for quicker searching*

By default, Windows only indexes certain areas of your PC's hard drive, and this doesn't include folders on external storage devices or those shared over a network.

To index a folder on an external storage device, either add the folder to Indexed Locations as shown in Figure 7-8, or add the folder to a Windows Library (contents of Libraries are automatically indexed). To add a folder to a library, right click or long tap it and choose "Include in Library".

You can also index the contents of a shared network folder when it's stored on a Windows server. If it is, you should be able to right click or long tap the network folder in File Explorer and choose "Always available offline". (Offline files are automatically indexed as well.) You can also add a networked folder to a library via the method described earlier.

Be aware that adding too many folders to the index can slow down your PC's performance, often noticeably. For this reason, it's preferable that you limit the number of folders that you add to the index, and instead store your files in areas that Windows indexes by default.

Click or tap the Advanced button in Figure 7-8 to relocate or rebuild the index as well as specify additional indexing options.

# Searching in Windows 10

Searching for files in Windows 10 is very similar to how it's done in Windows 8.1. In fact, when it comes to searching from File Explorer, it's actually exactly the same.

Unlike in Windows 8.1, however, Windows 10 doesn't allow you to initiate a quick file search using the Windows Key + F shortcut. In Windows 10, you can instead do this kind of search using the operating system's "Cortana" search feature.

To do a quick file search using Cortana, type your search term into the search box on the left side of the taskbar (it will either say "Ask me anything" or "Search the web and Windows"). This will display a list of best matches along with other search results from the Web (Figure 7-9). For complete search results, click or tap My Stuff to see the full list of matches, organized by category.

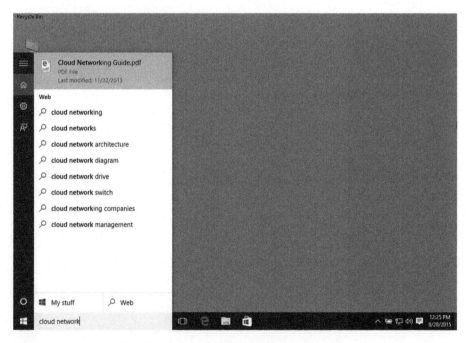

*Figure 7-9. Searching for files from the Windows 10 search box*

If you're using Windows 10 in Tablet mode, you won't see a search box, but you can still perform a search by tapping the circular Cortana icon.

# CHAPTER 8

# Cloud Storage and Transporting Files

One of the most common tasks associated with file management is transporting files from one computer to another. Very often this is because you're trying to share the file with someone such as a friend or family member, but it can also be because you want to copy files between different computers that you own.

The advent of cloud storage—that is, files stored online—makes sending files to others (or to yourself on another computer) much easier than via traditional methods such as email, burning discs, or using external storage devices (e.g., USB flash and hard drives).

In this chapter, we'll explore these methods in more detail and look at the advantages and disadvantages of each when it comes to getting files from Point A to Point B.

## Send in the Cloud

(apologies to Stephen Sondheim)

The trend toward ever larger and cheaper hard drives that's made the typical amount of PC storage grow over the years has also fueled the recent rise of cloud storage services. Dozens of companies now offer cloud storage, and at a basic level they all offer the same service—providing space on their server on which users can store their files.

As one of those users, once your files are "in the cloud" there are numerous benefits. First and foremost, when you upload files from your PC to cloud storage, you're automatically creating a backup of them (even though you shouldn't necessarily rely on cloud storage as your sole means of backup).

---

For more on backing up files, see Chapter 11.

---

In addition, most cloud storage services synchronize files between multiple PCs. Let's say that you have a desktop and a laptop. If you create or change a file on either computer that is synced to cloud storage, that new or changed file will be uploaded to your space on the online server and from there downloaded to the other computer. Hence, you'll always have the same files (and the same versions of files) on each computer. This mechanism can also be a handy way to transfer a large number of files between PCs at once—log into your cloud storage account on a new PC and you'll be able to easily, if not automatically, download your files to it.

Another advantage to cloud storage is how it facilitates sharing files with other people. The conventional way of doing so—by attaching the file to email—has numerous downsides, not the least of which is that the maximum size of files you can send is quite small by today's standards. (We'll go into more detail on that later.) But when your files are stored in the cloud, you don't actually need to send anything via email. Instead, you email someone an invitation with a link to your file in the cloud, which allows your recipient to access and download the file directly.

Not only does sharing a file via cloud storage save you the hassle of dealing with email attachment size limitations (many cloud storage services have file size limitations, too, but they're large enough to have little if any practical relevance), there are also other advantages. For example, you can decide whether you want someone to edit your shared file, or just view it.

## Cloud Cons

To be sure, storing files in the cloud has some downsides, too. For starters, you need a working Internet connection to get at them. This isn't usually a problem, but neither is it always a given. (Of course, if you are syncing cloud files with your PC, then you can still access the versions of the files on your own hard drive. These are typically referred to as "offline" or "local" copies.)

In addition, for privacy reasons you may not be very comfortable with the idea of your personal files being stored and managed by a third-party on some distant server, although in reality storing them on your own PC doesn't necessarily make them any more secure.

Finally, there's the cost. Although every cloud storage provider gives you a certain amount of storage capacity for free (between 2 and 15 GB is typical), that's not a lot compared to how much you can store on a typical PC, and you may find it insufficient unless your needs are relatively modest.

For more cloud storage space, you'll have to ante up for a monthly subscription, which typically runs between $2 and $20 per month depending on how much you need. Although the monthly fee amounts tend to be small, they can really add up when you're paying them year in and year out—indefinitely, to all intents and purposes.

Table 8-1 shows how much free space you get with some of the most popular cloud storage providers, along with the cost and capacity of the paid upgrade tiers.

***Table 8-1.*** *How much free and optional paid storage is available from major cloud storage services*

| Provider | Free | 1st paid upgrade (monthly) | 2nd paid upgrade (monthly) | 3rd paid upgrade (monthly) | 4th paid upgrade (monthly) |
|---|---|---|---|---|---|
| Microsoft OneDrive | 15 GB | 100 GB, $2 | 200 GB, $4 | 1 TB, $7 | n/a |
| Google Drive | 15 GB | 100 GB, $2 | 1 TB, $10 | 10 TB, $100 | 20 TB, $200 |
| Dropbox | 2 GB | 1TB, $10 | N/A | N/A | N/A |

Please note that these figures pertain to the consumer/personal versions of these services; capacities and pricing for business versions may be different. Also, figures were accurate at the time that this book was written, but as prices and capacities tend to change periodically (usually the former goes down and the latter goes up), consult the following links for the most current information:

Microsoft OneDrive

https://onedrive.live.com/about/en-us/plans/

Google Drive

https://support.google.com/drive/answer/2375123?hl=en

Dropbox

https://www.dropbox.com/plans?trigger=homepagefoot

## ADDING "FREE" STORAGE

Many cloud storage providers let you rack up extra storage in various ways other than having to pay for it (at least not explicitly). This may include higher free storage amounts only for certain file types (e.g., pictures), referring other people to the service, participating in promotions, or buying/subscribing to other products. For example, Microsoft includes 1 TB of OneDrive space with an annual subscription to their Office 365 productivity suite.

Be sure to check the fine print when redeeming such deals, as the bump up in space is often temporary. If you fill up on extra space that has an expiration date, at some point you'll have to choose between paying the rent or moving out of the apartment.

# Sharing via the Cloud

Now that we've gotten cloud storage basics out of the way, let's look at how to share a file that you're storing in the cloud.

Even if you've never used it before, there's a good chance that you already have a cloud storage account (and perhaps several). For example, if you have a Microsoft email account (one ending in either outlook.com or one of its precursors, hotmail.com or live.com), then you already have a OneDrive account. Similarly, if you have a Gmail account, then you also have a Google Drive account.

For the purposes of this book, we'll focus mainly on sharing files via Microsoft's OneDrive because this is the type of account that you're most likely to have as a Windows user. (For example, you need a Microsoft account in order to download apps—even free ones—from the company's Windows Store.) We'll also touch on on how to share files via Google Drive and Dropbox, as those services are popular as well.

---

For more on the benefits of using a Microsoft account with Windows, see Chapter 4.

---

## OneDrive (in Windows 8.1)

Assuming that you've logged in with a Microsoft Account, when you open File Explorer in Windows 8.1 (we'll talk about Windows 10 in a moment) you'll see OneDrive listed toward the top of the left pane. Tap or click on OneDrive, and the right pane will show all of the files and folders stored there.

To share a file (or folder), right click or long tap the item, select Share with, then OneDrive (Figure 8-1).

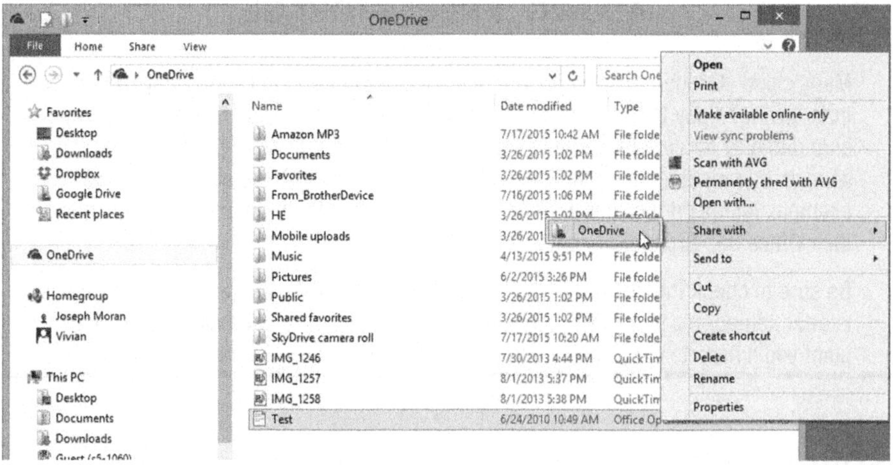

***Figure 8-1.*** *From File Explorer, right click or long tap a file or folder in OneDrive to display the Share with option*

Next, an Internet Explorer window will automatically open (or a different browser will if IE isn't your default) showing a screen similar to the one in Figure 8-2. Type in your recipient's email address (if sending to multiple people, separate addresses with either a comma or semicolon) and provide an explanatory note if desired.

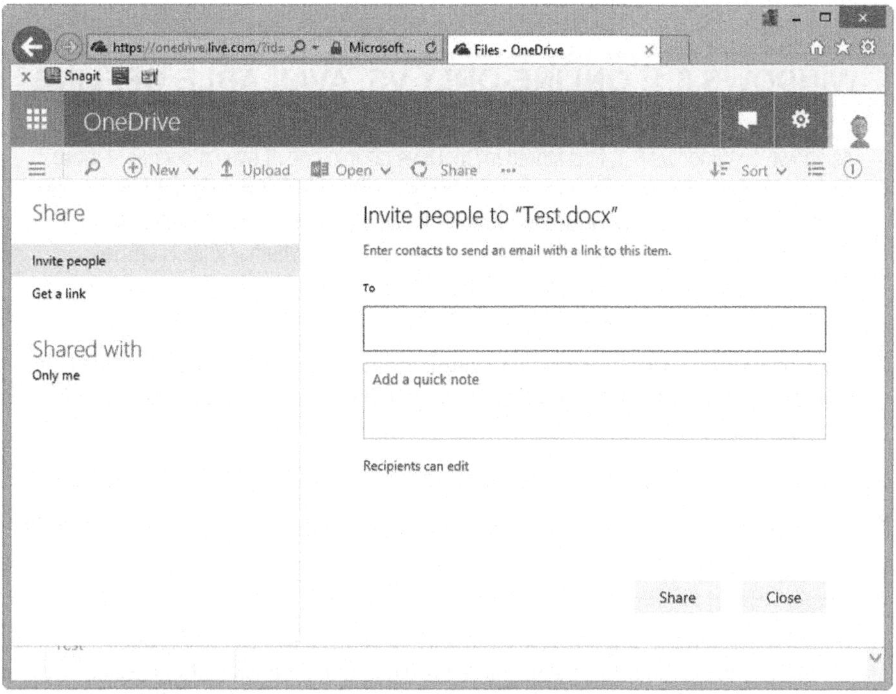

***Figure 8-2.*** *To invite someone to share the file, provide the email address of your recipient*

Wondering about the SkyDrive camera roll as shown in Figure 8-1? SkyDrive is what OneDrive used to be called before the name was changed as a result of a trademark settlement in early 2014. If you set up your account before the name change, you may still see this folder labeling as well.

As for the camera roll, this is a special OneDrive folder that you configure to automatically upload photos and videos from your smartphone or tablet (Windows, Android, or Apple) and, optionally, sync them to your PC(s).

To do this, download the OneDrive app from your smartphone/tablet's app store and follow the prompts to upload and sync your photos.

If you want your recipient to be able to edit the file as well as view it, click the Recipients can edit link to expose additional options.

To disseminate a file more widely than to a handful of people you know (e.g., post to a blog or social media), click or tap Get a Link (in the left pane under the Share heading) and choose your options. These include the ability to post directly to services such as Facebook, Twitter, or LinkedIn.

## WINDOWS 8.1: ONLINE-ONLY VS. AVAILABLE OFFLINE

As shown on Windows 8.1, files stored in OneDrive fall into one of two categories—those that exist only in cloud storage (online-only) and those that also exist on your PC (available offline). Depending on how (or whether) you've used OneDrive in the past, you may see both types of files when viewing them in File Explorer. To see whether a file is online-only or available offline, check the Availability column to the right of the file name, date modified, and size; you may have to scroll horizontally to see it.

If you're looking at files in a view that doesn't show details (e.g., icons only), you can still check the status of a file by selecting it—the bottom of the window will report its availability.

---

Windows doesn't display the online/offline status of folders; you need to open the folder to view the status of the files inside.

---

Windows 8.1 handles OneDrive Files this way so that you can use File Explorer to browse and search for files that you're storing in OneDrive without those files actually having to take up space on your PC (which might be limited). This caused confusion among some users, who may have thought that a file's appearance in File Explorer meant that it was located on the PC. The upshot is that at a glance you may think you have a local copy of a file only to find out later that you really don't (and if for whatever reason you don't have an Internet connection when you make the discovery, there's no way to get to the file).

Microsoft (wisely) choose to change the way that OneDrive files are handled in Windows 10 (more on that in a moment), but suffice it to say that if you're using Windows 8.1 and want to be certain that you have a local copy of a file or folder, be sure that the folder is set to Available offline. To change an item from online-only to available offline, right click or long tap it in File Explorer and choose that option from the menu, as shown in Figure 8-3. The selected file/folder will begin downloading to your PC' you'll immediately see the Availability listing change and the item's icon will display two (quite subtle) rotating arrows. Those arrows will disappear once the item finishes downloading, so be sure not to disconnect from the Internet before that happens. Depending on on the size and number of items involved and the speed of your connection, downloading could take several minutes, several hours, or more.

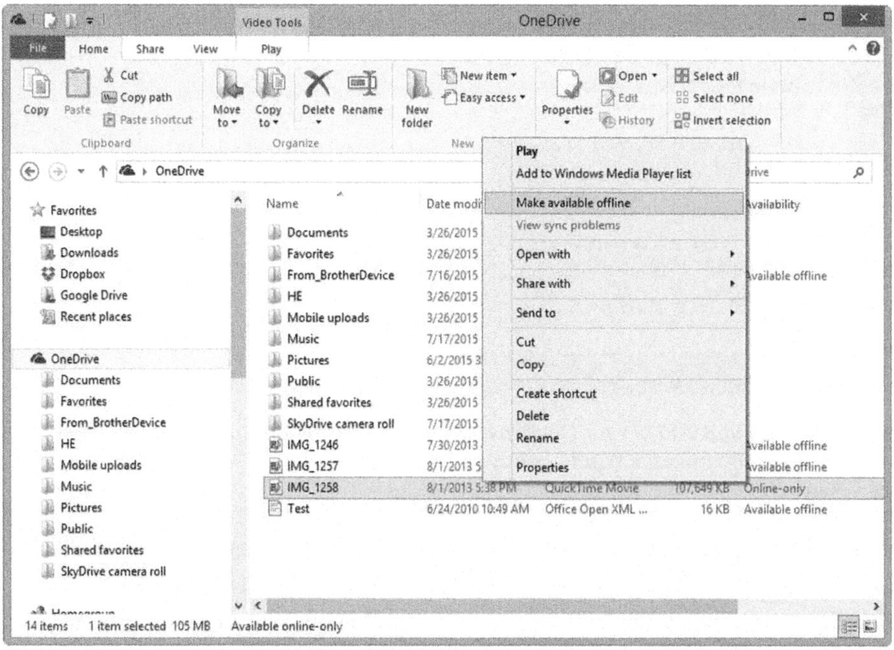

**Figure 8-3.** *To make a OneDrive file/folder available offline or online-only, right click or tap it and choose the appropriate option*

Incidentally, if you're running low on disk space, you can also switch a file/folder from available offline to online-only via the same method.

Finally, to change **every** OneDrive file and folder from online-only to available offline (or vice versa), locate the OneDrive settings icon in the Windows tray at the lower left, as shown in Figure 8-4. It looks like two white clouds. Right click or long tap it, choose Settings, and either check the box labeled Make all files available even when this PC isn't connected to the Internet or click/tap the button labeled Make all files online-only. If you don't see the OneDrive icon, click or tap the triangle to display it.

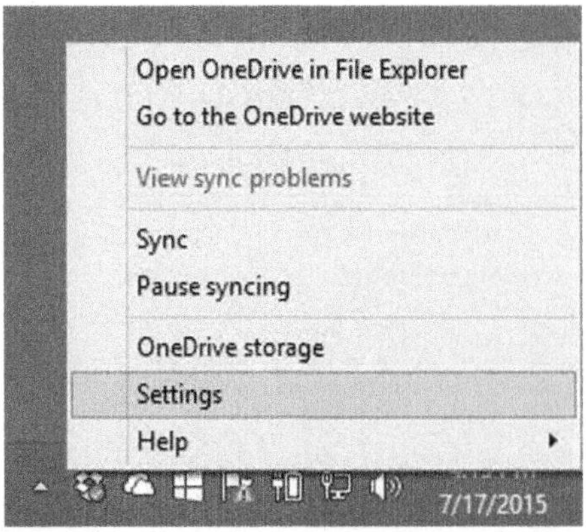

*Figure 8-4. To make all of your OneDrive files/folders online-only or available offline, use OneDrive Settings from the Windows tray*

If you're having problems with OneDrive in Windows 8.1 (e.g., it doesn't appear in File Explorer, etc.), Microsoft's OneDrive troubleshooter may be able to fix the problem. You can download the troubleshooter from windows.microsoft.com/en-us/windows-8/onedrive-troubleshooter. **(Note that at the time this book was written, this troubleshooter did not work with Windows 10.)**

Also, for general information about OneDrive, see the following link:

windows.microsoft.com/en-us/windows-8/onedrive-app-faq

# OneDrive (in Windows 10)

Microsoft changed how OneDrive is handled in Windows 10.

In Windows 10, you will ONLY see items that have been synced to your PC (i.e., you won't see files or folders that exist only in the cloud). Which items will be synced depends on the choices you made when you set up OneDrive on Windows 10 for the first time (or possibly what was already synced in Windows 8.1 when you upgraded).

In any event, to change what your Windows 10 PC syncs with OneDrive, right click or long tap on any OneDrive file or folder and select Choose OneDrive folders to sync to specify which folders you want to sync, or to sync all of them (Figure 8-5). If you don't yet have any files in OneDrive, you can reach this via the system tray, as previously described for Windows 8.1.

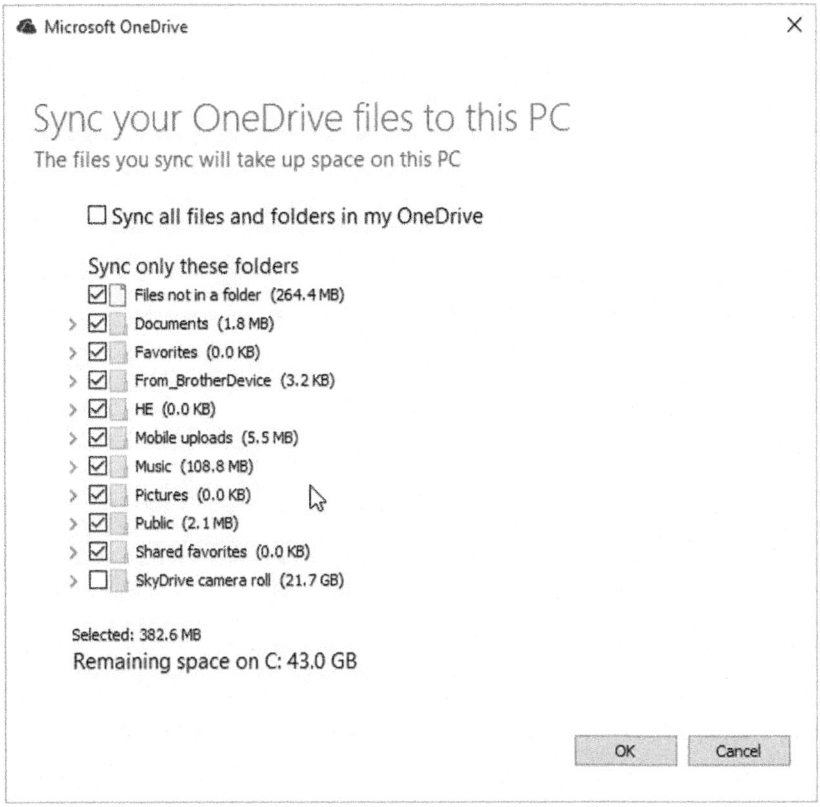

*Figure 8-5.* Unlike Windows 8.1, Windows 10 only displays those OneDrive files and folders that you've chosen to sync with the PC

As of this writing, Microsoft was planning a future update to Windows 10 that would handle OneDrive file syncing more like Windows 8.1.

By the way, this isn't the only change to OneDrive in Windows 10. Although you still share a OneDrive file from File Explorer by right clicking or long tapping it, when you do so (Figure 8-6), you'll see more than just a solitary Share option.

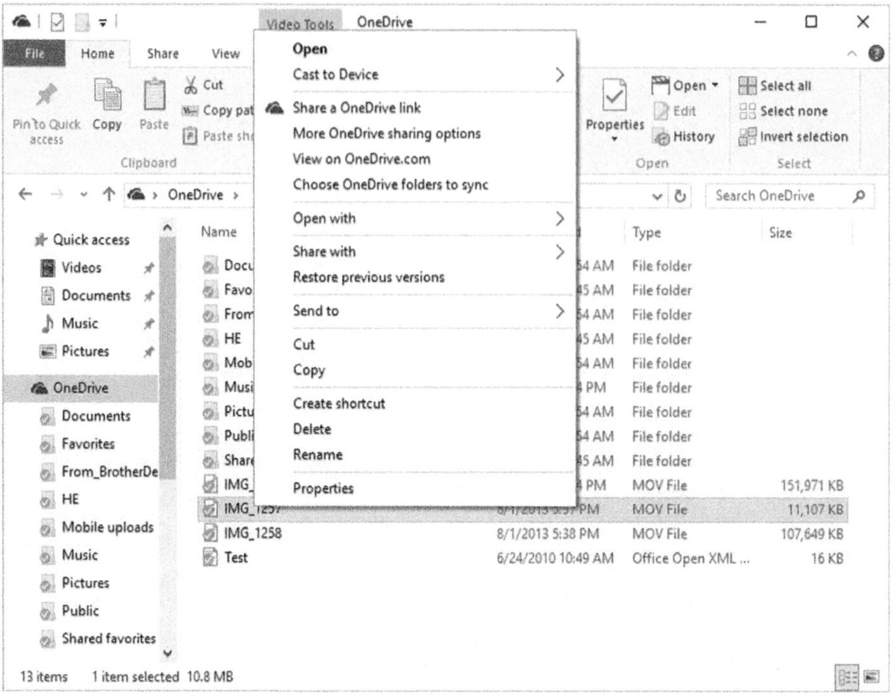

**Figure 8-6.** *Windows 10's File Explorer offers more OneDrive sharing options than Windows 8.1*

When you select the first option, Share a OneDrive link, you'll receive a notification that a link to your file was created and saved to your clipboard, ready for you to copy to a message or post (Figure 8-7).

**Figure 8-7.** *Windows 10's notification that a link to your shared file is ready*

Choose More OneDrive sharing options instead, and you'll be taken to the same kind of webpage shown in Figure 8-2, where you can specify email recipients and, if desired, what kind of access they'll have to the file. Lastly, the View on OneDrive.com option will open the copy of the file from cloud storage rather than from your PC. Choosing this option will launch the file in a Web browser window. One of the reasons that you might want to do this is if your PC lacks the app that created the file. For example, viewing an .XLSX file will automatically open it in Excel Online, the Web-based version of the app (which is handy if the app isn't installed on your PC).

## Other Cloud Services

To interact with cloud storage services other than OneDrive via File Explorer, you'll need to download a service-specific piece of software. You'll find Google Drive at tools.google.com/dlpage/drive, and the one for Dropbox is available at www.dropbox.com/downloading?src=index.

Once the software is installed, you'll most likely be able to browse and access your files from File Explorer under the Favorites category, as shown in Figure 8-8.

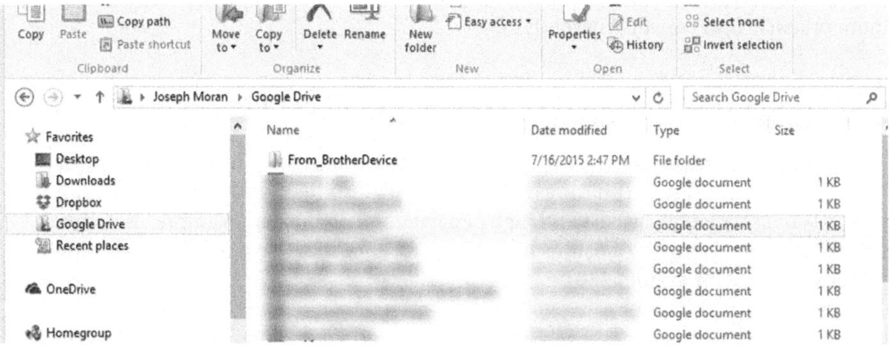

***Figure 8-8.*** *Install software from your cloud service provider to view and access stored files within File Explorer*

---

Always remember that if you're away from your own PC, you can still access your cloud-stored files directly from the provider's website. For the services discussed in this book, those links are:

Onedrive.live.com
Drive.google.com

www.dropbox.com

---

# Other Methods of Transporting Files

If you can't use the cloud to move or share your files—or you don't want to—you can still fall back on more conventional (albeit limiting) methods such as sending via email, aving to external storage devices, or burning to disc.

# Email

Attaching a file or files to email is a simple way to send someone something, but the limits placed on message size make it impractical to send large files—or a large number of files—this way. As of this writing, the maximum message size for Gmail or AOL email accounts is 25 MB, and for Microsoft accounts (outlook.com and Hotmail.com), it's a mere 10 MB. This is usually sufficient for sending documents or perhaps a handful of low-resolution photos, but if you try to send a handful of high-resolution photos or even a single high-definition video file you'll most likely bump up against that limit.

For this reason, sharing files via the cloud, as outlined earlier in this chapter, is a far more practical and convenient method.

# USB Flash Drives and Portable External Hard Drives

USB flash drives and external hard drives are a good choice for transporting large—or large numbers of—files (or sharing them, at least with someone close by). One important reason is the relatively low cost and high capacities available. For example, as of this writing an 8 GB Flash drive costs as little as $5 and a portable external 1 TB hard drive costs can be had for around $50.

---

Portable external hard drives (which are usually labeled as such) are smaller and lighter than "desktop" external drives and don't require a separate AC power adapter like desktop drives do. They get power from the USB port, which makes using them quite convenient.

---

The small physical size and high capacity of USB flash and portable external drives can be a double-edged sword, however, as the devices are susceptible to loss or even theft. For this reason, it's a good idea to consider encryption when storing particularly sensitive files on these devices. (See Chapter 12 for more on encryption.)

## THE "FILE TOO LARGE" ERROR

When copying a very large file to a USB flash or external hard drive (but especially to the former), you may encounter an error message informing you that "the file is too large for the destination" even when there is seemingly plenty of space available.

This error usually occurs because you were trying to copy a file larger than 4 GB in size (most likely a video file) to a storage device formatted with the FAT32 file system, which doesn't allow file sizes larger than 4 GB. More accurately, most USB flash drives come out of their packaging formatted using a file system called exFAT (in order to support both Windows and Mac systems), but Windows PCs see such devices as being formatted with the older FAT32 file system.

Fortunately, there's a relatively easy way to fix the problem, which is to reformat the USB flash drive with a different file system called NTFS. (Most external hard drives come formatted with NTFS.)

To verify what kind of file system a device is using, right click or long tap it in File Explorer, then choose Properties and consult the line labeled File System (Figure 8-9). To reformat a drive, right click or long tap it, choose Format, then select NTFS under File System before clicking or tapping Start (Figure 8-10).

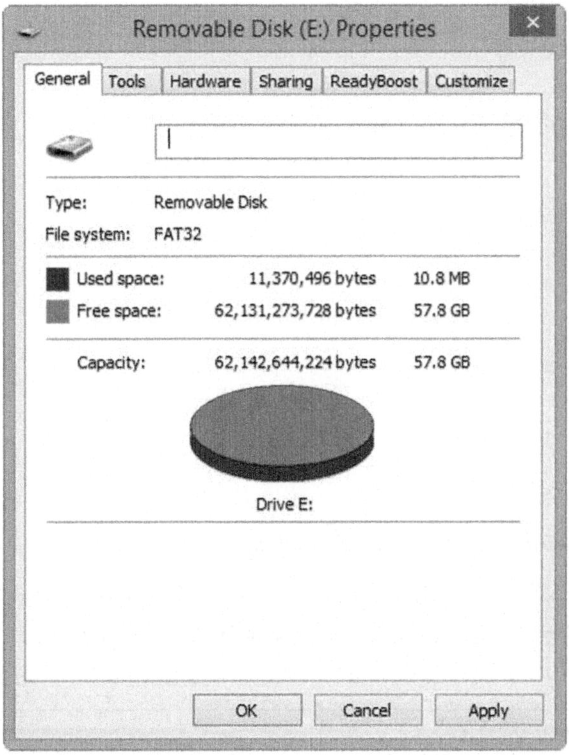

***Figure 8-9.*** *Check the properties of a drive to see what type of file system it uses*

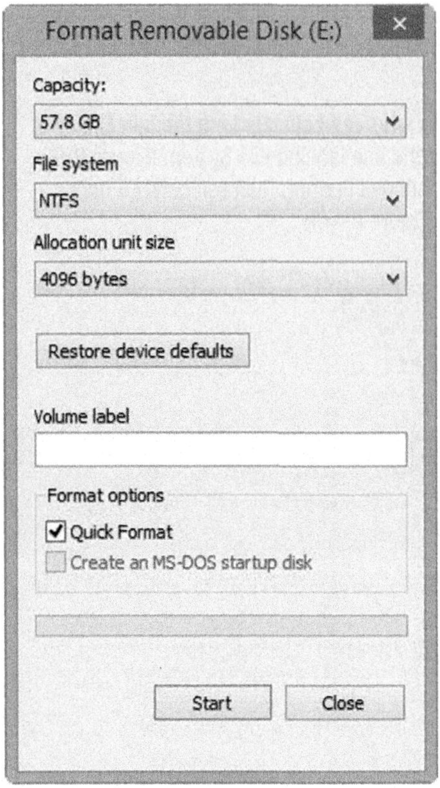

**Figure 8-10.** *Right click or long tap a drive and choose Format to reformat it as NTFS*

---

Formatting will erase everything that's stored on a drive, so be sure to check for anything important before doing so.

---

For more on the differences between the NTFS and FAT32 file systems, see:

windows.microsoft.com/en-us/windows7/comparing-ntfs-and-fat32-file-systems

# Copying Files to Optical Disc

Copying—also known as "burning"—files to an optical disc (e.g., a DVD) was once a common way of transporting and sharing files, but it's rapidly falling out of favor for the following reasons:

> USB flash and hard drives are relatively inexpensive and offer much higher capacities than optical discs

> Transferring files to a flash or hard drive is both a simpler and quicker process than burning them to a disc

> More and more PCs (particularly small lightweight laptops and convertible/hybrid tablet-style systems) do not include optical disc drives

That said, burning files to disc can sometimes be a cost-effective way to archive data (i.e., put it into long-term storage), because the price of an individual disc can be much less expensive than a USB flash drive. The amount that you can store on a disc depends on the kind of drive you have and the type of blank discs (also known as media) you use with them.

Some common types are listed in Table 8-2.

***Table 8-2.*** *Common DVD/BD types and capacities*

| Disc Type | Abbreviation | Capacity (GB) | Approximate Price |
|---|---|---|---|
| DVD Recordable, DVD Rewritable | DVD-R, DVD+R DVD-RW, DVD +RW | 4.7 | $15 per 50 discs (recordable), $20 per 25 discs (rewritable) |
| DVD Recordable Dual Layer | DVD-R DL, DVD+R DL | 8.5 | $30 per 50 discs |
| Blu-ray Disc Recordable, Blu-ray Disc Recordable Erasable | BD-R, BD-RE | 25 | $40 per 50 discs (recordable), $30 per 20 discs (rewritable) |
| Blu-ray Disc Recordable, Blu-ray Disc Recordable Erasable (Dual Layer) | BD-R DL, BD-RE DL | 50 | $100 per 50 discs (recordable), $25 per 5 discs (recordable erasable) |

To get the capacities listed in Table 8-2, the blank discs you use must match the capabilities of your drive (e.g., dual-layer discs on a dual-layer drive). Also notice how disc prices increase significantly as capacity rises, from about 30 cents per disc for 4.7 GB DVD recordable media to $5 per disc for 50 GB Blu-ray recordable erasable media.

■ ■ ■

# CHAPTER 9

# Managing Open Files and Windows

An important aspect of good File Management is having the ability to easily access the files you need and, moreover, being able to efficiently navigate through lots of open files.

In this chapter, we'll outline various ways to streamline access to commonly used files, how to switch between multiple open files, and how to organize open files on screen.

---

■ **Note**    that the information in this chapter pertains to Windows 8.1 and/or Windows 10 running in Desktop mode, which uses a conventional interface with icons and windows rather than one with tiles and full screen apps designed primarily for touch-based input. A good rule of thumb: if you see the Taskbar described here, you're almost certainly in desktop mode; if you don't, you're probably not.

---

## Pin Apps to the Taskbar

One of the best things that you can do to facilitate easy access to your most frequently used files is to pin the app that's associated with them to the Windows Taskbar—the small horizontal strip of real estate at the bottom of the screen when you're using either Windows 8.1 or Windows 10 in desktop mode.

Windows pins several apps to the Taskbar by default. These include Internet Explorer, File Explorer, and Windows Store. But you can also pin your own apps to the Taskbar as well. To pin an app to the Taskbar, search for it from the Start menu, then right click or long tap the item and choose Pin to Taskbar, as shown in Figure 9-1.

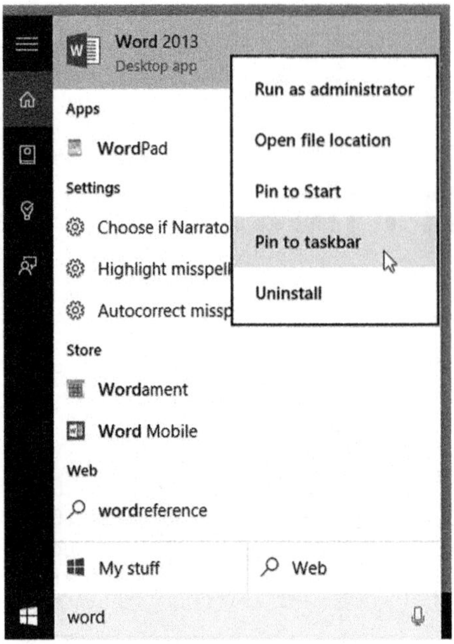

**Figure 9-1.** *Pinning an app to the taskbar in Windows 10*

The Start Menu in Windows 8.1 looks different from that in Figure 9-1, but the process to search for and pin an app is the same.

After you've pinned an app to the Taskbar, you'll see that its icon takes up residence at the bottom of the screen. In Figure 9-2, for example, we've pinned Microsoft Word, Microsoft Excel, and Adobe Reader to the Windows 10 taskbar.

**Figure 9-2.** *Apps pinned to the Windows 10 Taskbar*

All apps appear on the Taskbar while they're open even if they've not been pinned, but the benefit to pinning an app is that it will appear on the Taskbar even when it's NOT open. To pin an open app to the Taskbar so that it will remain there even after it is closed, right click or long tap the app's icon and choose Pin this program to taskbar.

# Recent and Pinned Files

Once an app is pinned to the Taskbar, accessing files gets a lot more convenient. Right click or long tap a pinned app and a "Recent" menu (also known as a Jump List) will pop up, giving you one-click access to the files that you recently used with that app. (Some apps, such as File Explorer and Windows Media Player, use the label "Frequent" rather than "Recent".)

Even better, you can keep any recently accessed file even closer at hand by pinning it to the Jump List.To pin a file to a Jump List, hover the mouse cursor over a file. You'll see a pin icon appear to the right of its name. Click it and the file selected will appear in a new "Pinned" list above the list of recent files. Repeat the process to unpin a pinned file (Figure 9-3).

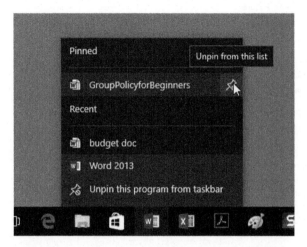

*Figure 9-3. Pinned and Recent files for Microsoft Word*

## PINNING FOLDERS AND FILES TO THE TASKBAR

Windows makes it easy to pin files—and even folders—to the Taskbar even if they haven't been opened recently. To pin a file or folder to the Taskbar, find the item in File Explorer, then click or tap and hold and drag it down to *an empty area* of the Taskbar, letting it go once you see the Pin to... label appear. (This label will vary depending on which kind of item you are trying to pin.)

Case in point: if you've chosen to pin a folder, it will be pinned to File Explorer. If you've selected a file, it will be pinned to the default app for that file type; if that app isn't already pinned to your Taskbar, pinning the file will automatically pin the app along with it.

# Pinning Apps and Folders to the Start Menu

Another way to make accessing your files more convenient is to pin frequently used apps or folders to the Start Menu, which effectively creates a shortcut to the item in the form of a tile. To pin an app to the Start Menu, right click or long tap it as shown in Figure 9-1 but choose the Pin to Start option.

Pinning an app to the Start Menu isn't quite as useful as pinning it to the Taskbar because it doesn't provide access to a Jump List of Recent or Pinned files for that app. By contrast, pinning a *folder* to the Start Menu can provide easy access to its contents.

To pin a folder to the Start Menu, right click or long tap it in File Explorer and select Pin to Start (Figures 9-4 and 9-5).

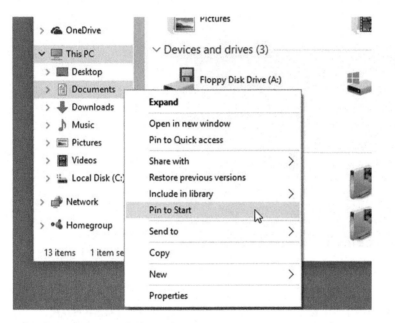

*Figure 9-4. Pinning a folder to the Start menu ...*

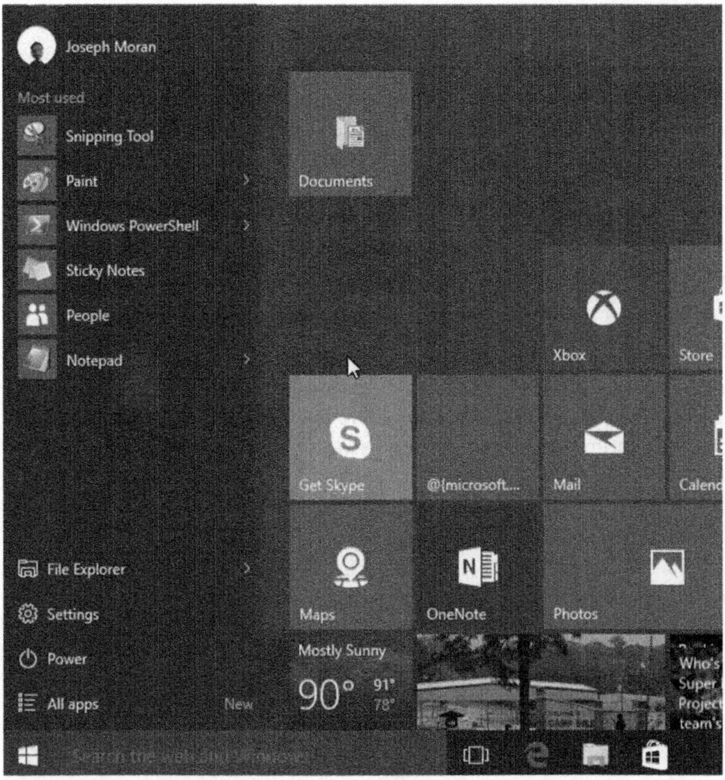

***Figure 9-5.*** *... and how it looks (in Windows 10) when complete*

Once you've pinned an app or folder to the Start menu in either Windows 8.1 or Windows 10, you may resize it (right click or long tap and choose Resize) or drag it to another location in the menu.

# Switching Between Open Files in an App

You've probably experienced the frustration of having countless files open in different windows and having difficulty finding a specific file or spending a lot time of jumping between different windows trying to find the particular file you want at that moment.

As we saw earlier, pinning apps and files to the Taskbar can make opening frequently used files a lot more convenient. But the Taskbar's usefulness doesn't end there; it can also streamline the process of moving back and forth between different open apps, files, or windows, especially when you have multiple files/windows open in the same app. Here's how.

## Using the Taskbar

An app's icon on the Taskbar gives you considerable visibility and control over your open files. For starters, when you have a file open in a given app, its Taskbar item will appear highlighted. And if you have multiple files open in a given app, "stacked" (i.e., overlapping) buttons provide a visual indication of this.

---

To save space on the Taskbar, button stacking won't necessarily reflect how many files you have open in an app. For example, if you have five files open, you won't see five stacked buttons.

---

To see which file(s) are open in an app, click or tap the Taskbar button (or you can simply hover the mouse cursor over the button) to display thumbnails of all of the open files (Figure 9-6). Then, click or tap a thumbnail to bring that file's window to the foreground and close the thumbnails. You can also use the X in the right corner of a thumbnail to close the corresponding file. If you're using a mouse, hovering the cursor over the thumbnails without clicking on them will allow you to view each file windows before deciding which one to switch to.

***Figure 9-6.*** *Click or tap an app's Taskbar button for thumbnail views of all of its open files*

---

Want to close all the files open in an app? Right click or long tap the Taskbar button and choose Close all windows—if any files need to be saved, you'll be prompted to do that.

---

# Switching Between Any Open File or App

Using an app's Taskbar button lets you conveniently view and switch between files that are open in that particular app. But what if you want to switch between the files that are open in ALL of your apps?

An easy way to do this is via the ALT+TAB key combination. To use it, hold down ALT then press TAB (but continue to hold down ALT). A box will appear showing individual thumbnail views for each open file or app window, plus one for the Windows Desktop (Figure 9-7). As you continue to hold ALT, press TAB repeatedly to select each successive thumbnail, which will bring the corresponding window to the foreground. Once you've you've found the file or app you want, release the ALT and TAB keys.

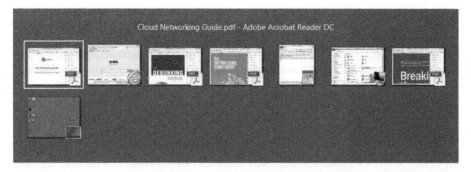

***Figure 9-7.*** *Use ALT+TAB to view and switch between all open files and apps (Windows 8.1)*

If you find holding down ALT + TAB together too cumbersome, another option is to press ALT+TAB+CTRL simultaneously. This will keep the thumbnails on screen without the need to hold down any keys. With this method, use TAB or the left/right arrow keys to swtich between thumbnails, ENTER to select one, and ESC to close the thumbnail view (or use the mouse to switch between and select thumbnails).

---

When you use ALT+TAB or ALT+TAB+CTRL in Windows 10, the thumbnail view looks a little different than that shown in Figure 9-7. Thumbnail sizes will vary depending on how many there are (so fewer thumbnails = bigger thumbnails), and there is no thumbnail for the desktop.

---

# Viewing Multiple Files Simultaneously

When you have many files and/or apps, open at once, the Taskbar and ALT+TAB methods that we've outlined so far let you hone in on one particular file of interest. But what if you want to see two (or more) files without one file's windows obstructing your view of another?

This is where Windows Snap feature comes in. Let's say that you have two files open and you want to be able to work on them at the same time. With Snap, you can easily arrange them side-by-side so that each takes up exactly half of your screen.

# Snap (Windows 8.1)

To Snap a pair of files, click or tap the title bar at the top of a file and drag it to either the left or right edge of the screen, then let go once you see the faint outline of that half of the screen, as shown in Figure 9-8. Then repeat the process for another file on the opposite side of the screen and you'll wind up with two adjacent files, as shown in Figure 9-9.

***Figure 9-8.*** *Snapping a window to the right side of the screen*

**Figure 9-9.** *Two windows snapped side by side*

To unsnap a file window and return it to its original size and position, just double click/tap its title bar, or drag the window away from the edge of the screen until it returns to its original size.

## OTHER USEFUL SNAPS

You can snap windows in a couple of other useful ways that don't necessarily facilitate viewing multiple files simultaneously. For example, drag a file window to the top edge of the screen to make it full screen. To maximize a window's height but not its width, place the cursor along the top or bottom edge of the window (the cursor will become a vertical arrow), then click and drag upward or downward (as appropriate) until you reach the top or bottom of the screen.

# Snap and Snap Assist (Windows 10)

The Snap feature includes several enhancements in Windows 10. For starters, if you have multiple file windows open and snap one of them to either edge of your screen, Windows 10 will automatically assume that you want to snap another one to the opposite side as well, where it will display thumbnail views of your other open windows (Figure 9-10). This feature is called Snap Assist; click or tap any thumbnail to snap that window to the remaining half.

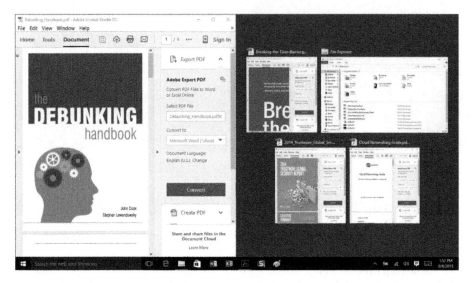

***Figure 9-10.*** *With Snap Assist, snap a file to one side of the screenin Windows 10 then choose which thumbnail to snap to the opposite side*

Windows 10 also allows you to snap a file window not just to the left and right edges but into all four corners of the screen. The process works much like it does in Windows 8.1 and as shown in Figure 9-8, except that you drag the window into a corner until you see that corner highlighted. (Snap Assist works in this mode as well.) Note that in Windows 10 you can mix and match your snaps—for example, you can snap a window to one side of the screen and two more to the opposite corners.

## Snap Keyboard Shortcuts

Snapping windows using a mouse or finger can sometimes be imprecise, so here are some simple keyboard shortcuts that can make the tasks a lot easier.

| Action | Keyboard Shortcut |
| --- | --- |
| Snap to left edge | Windows Logo+ left arrow |
| Snap to right edge | Windows Logo+right arrow |
| Snap to upper left quadrant (Windows 10 only) | Windows Logo+ left arrow THEN Windows Logo + up arrow |
| Snap to lower left quadrant (Windows 10 only) | Windows Logo+ left arrow THEN Windows LOGO + down arrow |
| Snap to upper Right quadrant (Windows 10 only) | Windows Logo+right arrow THEN Windows LOGO + up arrow |
| Snap to upper right quadrant (Windows 10 only) | Windows Logo+right arrow THEN Windows LOGO + down arrow |

# Task View and Virtual Desktops (Windows 10)

Windows 10 includes a couple of new features to help you keep your open files organized.

The first is called Task View, which you can access via the corresponding button on the Taskbar (Figure 9-11) or by pressing Windows + TAB.

***Figure 9-11.*** *The Task View button on the Taskbar*

Activating Task View offers a way to view and switch between all your open windows much like the ALT+TAB and ALT+TAB+CTRL methods described earlier (and, like the latter, it doesn't require you to hold down any keys). But what really makes Task View useful is that you can combine it with Virtual Desktops, a feature that lets you group related files, windows, or apps together into separate desktops to limit the number of windows open in front of you at a given time.

When you activate Task View, you'll see thumbnails of your open windows, along with a plus sign labeled "New desktop" at the lower right corner of the screen. To transfer a window to a new desktop, drag and drop it onto New Desktop. You'll now see Desktop 1 and Desktop 2 thumbnails at the bottom center of the screen (your original desktop is Desktop 1) (Figure 9-12). You can then drag and drop remaining open windows down to your existing desktops or create yet more desktops. When you're done, click or tap the thumbnail for the Virtual Desktop you to which you want to return.

113

***Figure 9-12.*** *Windows organized into two Virtual Desktops*

Once your windows are organized into Virtual Desktops, you can use Task View to switch between them at any time. (Another way to switch between Virtual Desktops is Windows+CTRL+left or right arrow.)

To close a virtual desktop, click the arrow to the upper right of its thumbnail in Task View or press Windows+CTRL+F4 to close the currently selected Virtual Desktop.

When you close a Virtual Desktop, its files/windows/apps don't close; they're automatically transferred to the previous desktop. For example, close Desktop 3 and its items are transferred to Desktop 2, and so on.

---

When you are using Virtual Desktops, ALT+TAB and the Taskbar only show the windows open in that Virtual Desktop. If you want to change this behavior so that you can view windows open across all desktops, click or tap the Start button, then Settings, System, and finally, Multitasking. Then modify the options listed under Virtual desktops.

---

# CHAPTER 10

■ ■ ■

# Sharing Files on a Home Network

If your household is like many, it probably has a home network with multiple PCs on it, and at some point you're probably going to want to share files between those PCs.

In this chapter, we'll look at three different ways to accomplish this:

Create or Join a Windows HomeGroup

Share an external storage device via a home Wi-Fi router

Use a Network Attached Storage (NAS) device as a home server

Before we get into the details of these different methods, it's worth noting that if you use a cloud storage service to store files online and sync them across multiple computers, you likely also have the ability to share those files—not just with others on your home network but with anyone that has an Internet connection. For more on how to share files via the cloud, see Chapter 9.

## Creating or Joining a HomeGroup

If your home network includes multiple PCs, Windows' built-in HomeGroup feature offers an easy way to share files between them. When you set up a HomeGroup, the user of each PC that becomes a member can decide what they want—or don't want—to share and whether they want others to be able to change the files to which they've been given access. Your HomeGroup will also be protected by a password to prevent uninvited PCs from joining it.

---

The HomeGroup feature is part of Windows 10, Windows 8.x, and Windows 7.

---

To create a HomeGroup, start by searching for "homegroup", then run HomeGroup and select the Create button. After a few moments you'll see a screen like the one shown in Figure 10-1; review the list of Libraries and other items and switch each one you want

115

to share from Off to On. Finally, make note of the password shown at the bottom of the screen (you may need to scroll to see it), because it will be required to join other PCs to the HomeGroup.

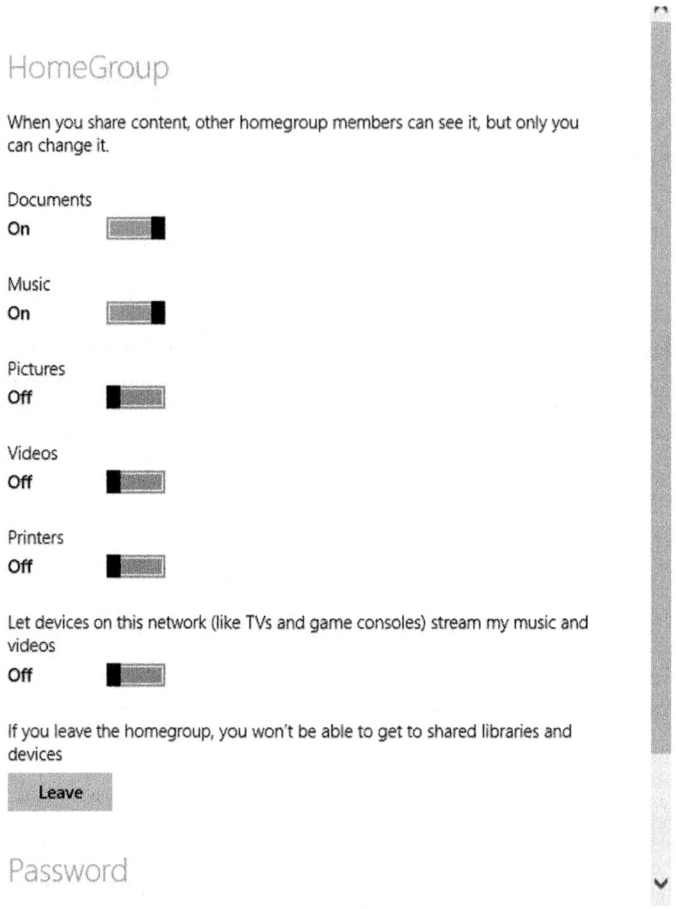

*Figure 10-1.  Select the items that you want to share and make note of the password shown, because other PCs will need it to join the HomeGroup and access your shared files*

There are a couple of things to keep in mind when setting up a HomeGroup. If someone else on your network's already created one, you won't be able to set up a new one; you will only be able to join the existing one (provided that you have the password).

It's also important to note that a HomeGroup is a group of PCs first and users second. This means that when someone creates or joins a HomeGroup on their PC, every user account on that PC (except for the Guest account) potentially becomes a member of the HomeGroup, but only the user who explicitly created or joined the HomeGroup will have his or her data shared (in accordance with the choices that they make as shown in Figure 10-1). Files from other user accounts on the PC won't be accessible to the HomeGroup unless each user makes their own sharing choices.

## Accessing Shared Files

Once you've shared items with a HomeGroup, others will be able to find those items via the File Explorer on any other PC that's also a member of the HomeGroup. To access shared HomeGroup files, open File Explorer and look along the left pane for the Homegroup heading (for some reason Microsoft switches from a capital to a lowercase "g" when referring to Homegroup in File Explorer). Depending on your version of Windows as well as other variables, you may find the Homegroup heading closer to the top or the bottom of the left pane.

Under the Homegroup heading, you'll see one or more names representing user accounts that have shared files with the HomeGroup. Click or tap the name in the left pane and you'll see what they've shared in the right pane (Figure 10-2). You can then double click or double tap an item to open it and browse for the files that you want.

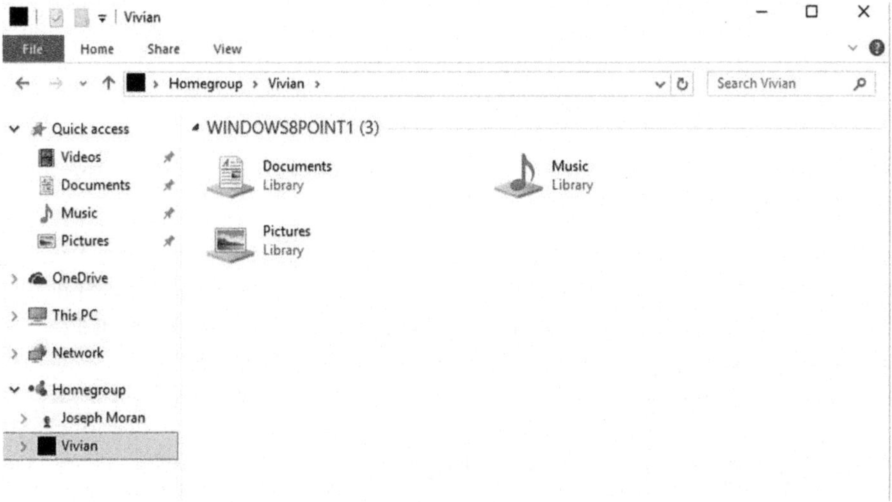

***Figure 10-2.*** *Click on a name under File Explorer's Homegroup heading to view and browse what they've shared*

## Changing HomeGroup Share Permissions

Libraries are shared with View access by default, which means that other users can see and browse what you've shared and open files but cannot change or delete anything. If you want to allow others to modify something that you've shared, you must first change the permissions for the shared item.

To change the permissions for a shared item, select it in File Explorer, tap or click the Share tab, then select **Homegroup (view and edit)** from the **Share with** group (Figure 10-3).

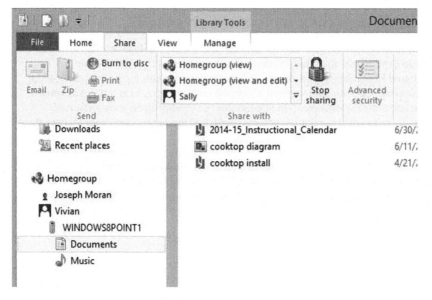

***Figure 10-3.*** *To change the default share permissions for an item, select it in File Explorer, click the Share tab, and choose HomeGroup (view and edit)*

---

If you see names listed in the **Share with** group (as shown in Figure 10-3), they refer to other user accounts on your PC. Sharing files with other users on a PC works much the same way as sharing with a HomeGroup; for more on this, see Chapter 4.

---

# Sharing Additional Files or Folders

In some cases, you may not want to share an entire Library but, rather, only a specific file or folder. Sharing a specific file or folder with a HomeGroup works just like changing the permissions of something that you've already shared—select the item, tap or click the Share tab, then choose either Homegroup (view) or Homegroup (view and edit) from the **Share with** group, depending on the kind of access that you want to provide (Figure 10-4).

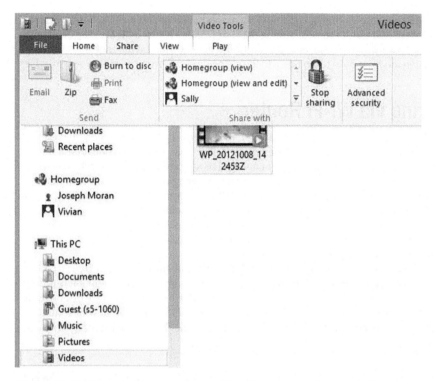

***Figure 10-4.*** *When sharing a new item with a HomeGroup, choose whether you want to provide view or view and edit access*

If you want to stop sharing a particular item—file, folder, or Library—with your HomeGroup, the easiest way to do so is to select the item from File Explorer, tap or click the Share tab, then tap or click the big padlock labeled **Stop sharing**. (If this is grayed out, you aren't sharing the item.)

## Leaving a HomeGroup

To leave a HomeGroup, return to the HomeGroup settings screen shown in Figure 10-1 and tap or click the **Leave** button.

---

If you can't quite remember what you're sharing with your HomeGroup, you don't have to check that from another PC. To see what you're sharing, just consult File Explorer on your own PC—look for your own name under HomeGroup.

---

HomeGroups are a convenient way to share files between multiple PCs, but they also have some drawbacks. Foremost among these drawbacks is that a PC must be on and on the home network for its files to be available. If a PC has been turned off, gone into sleep or hibernation mode, or been taken down to the coffee shop, you won't be able to access its files.

# Sharing via Wi-Fi Router

A good way to avoid these limitations is to share files from a central location, making them accessible via a device that by definition is always on and on the network. A home Wi-Fi router is just such a device, and many models sport USB ports to which you can connect an external storage device and share its contents with every PC on your network.

To be sure, not all Wi-Fi routers include a USB port for file sharing. Most inexpensive entry-level models don't offer one, but if your router cost more than $50 and was purchased within the last few years there's a good chance that it has one, so be sure to check. (Check all around the router—back, front, and sides—because USB ports aren't always easy to spot at a glance.)

If your router does have a USB port and its sharing feature is on by default (which is often the case) you may only need to plug in the storage device and wait for a few minutes before you can access it on your PC. You will find the device under the **Network** heading in File Explorer, often (although not always) named something similar to your router model number. For example, as shown in Figure 10-5, the storage device plugged into our Asus TM-AC1900 router appears as TM-AC1900-A018.

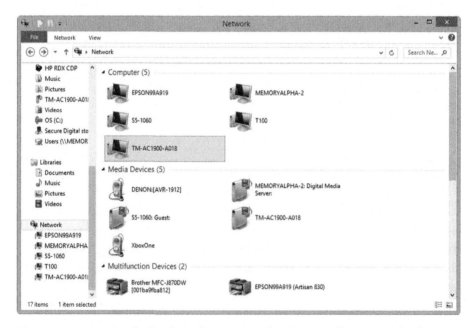

**Figure 10-5.** *A storage device plugged into a router's USB port will appear under the Network heading of File Explorer, often named similarly to the router model*

If you don't see the storage device appear within several minutes of plugging it in, you you may need to log into your router's administrative control panel to turn on the USB file-sharing feature.

Even if you can see your shared USB device without any further configuration, you may still want to log into your router because many allow you to control access to the files by creating usernames, passwords, and, as with HomeGroups, you can specify whether you want someone to have permission to only read or both read and write (i.e., change or delete) shared files.

Every router manufacturer has a different way of configuring USB file sharing, so we can't provide step-by-step instructions. As an example, Figure 10-6 shows an example of these settings on an Asus TM-AC1900 router.

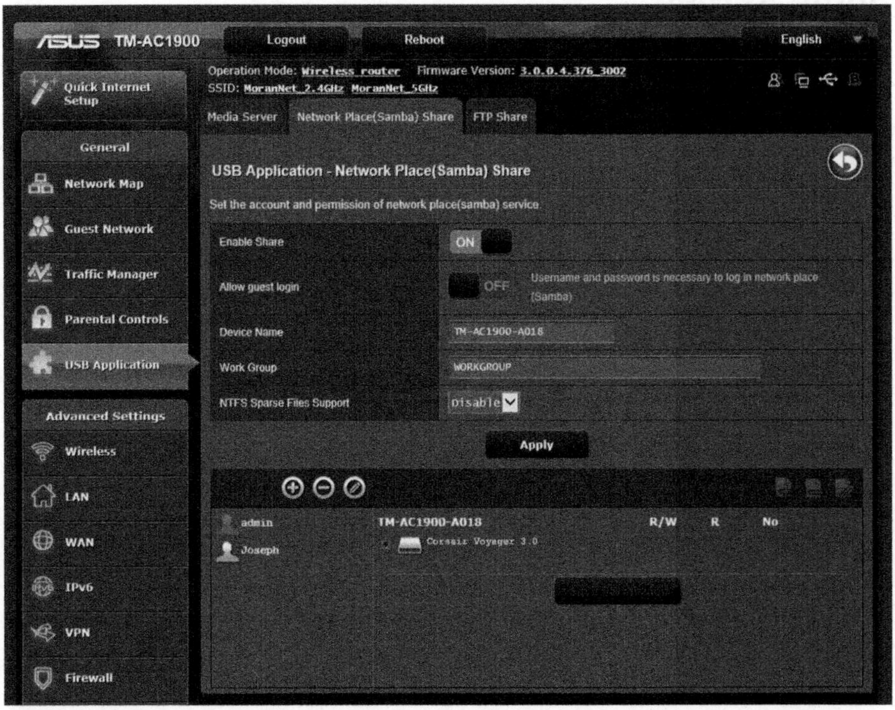

***Figure 10-6.*** *You can enable/disable USB file sharing and control access to files from a router's administrative control panel*

If your router has a USB 3.0 port—the documentation should specify, but USB 3.0 ports are usually blue and/or labeled "SS" (for SuperSpeed)—connect a USB 3.0 storage device for best performance (USB 3.0 is up to 10 times faster).

While sharing files via a router's USB port addresses the limitations of a HomeGroup, it has some drawbacks of its own. For example, many routers only have one USB port, which means that you can only share the contents of a single USB storage device. Also, there's no easy way to back up the contents of that device so that your data is protected in the event of a drive failure. If you want the ability to share truly large amounts of data—for example, a mammoth collection of videos, photographs, or music, for example—and be able to protect it from loss at the same time, you might want to consider buying a Network Attached Storage (NAS) device to use as a home server.

# Using a Network Attached Storage (NAS) as a Home Server

Network Attached Storage (NAS) devices are basically powerful yet compact computers, the main purpose of which is to store and share files with multiple PCs over a network. NAS devices connect directly to your home network via Ethernet cable (most don't use Wi-Fi because it isn't considered fast or reliable enough) and give you lots of capacity because they use multiple internal hard drives to store data. (Typical home NAS devices sport two, four, or even more drives.)

With the capacity of multiple drives on tap, NAS devices can use some of that space and a technology called RAID (Redundant Array of Independent Disks) to store a secondary copy of your data, ensuring that it can survive the failure of any one disk. For an extra level of protection, NAS devices can also be backed up to a USB-connected hard drive and/or to a cloud storage service.

As an added bonus, most NAS devices also give you the ability to stream or sync files with your PCs as well as remotely access files from outside your home from any device with an Internet connection (including, typically, a smartphone or tablet).

Home NAS devices are available from a variety of manufacturers and come in all shapes, sizes, and prices, although very capable basic models can be had for just a few hundred dollars. (Figure 10-7 shows the two-hard drive WD My Cloud Mirror, which as of this writing retails for $300.)

***Figure 10-7.*** *NAS devices such as the WD My Cloud mirror use multiple internal hard disks to store, share, and protect your data*

To learn more about NAS devices, see the following links:

Drobo

www.drobo.com/storage-products/drobo/

Netgear

www.netgear.com/home/products/connected-storage/readynas.aspx#tab-overview

QNAP

www.qnap.com/i/useng/product/items_by_series.php?CA=3

Seagate

www.seagate.com/products/network-attached-storage/home-network/personal-cloud/

WD (Western Digital)

www.wdc.com/en/products/personalcloud/consumer/

---

A NAS server or external storage connected to a Wi-Fi router can be a good place to store File History (or use any other backup method/software) for multiple PCs on a network. For more on how to use File History to backup your files, see Chapter 11.

---

# CHAPTER 11

■ ■ ■

# Backing Up Your Files

It doesn't matter how many bells and whistles your PC has or how much it costs—the true value of a PC isn't really in its features or price tag, it's in all of the data that you've stored on it. Whether it's documents you spent countless hours creating and editing, a vast digital music collection painstakingly built up over many years, or thousands of photos and videos that carry priceless family memories, it's absolutely crucial that you safeguard that data by backing it up. If you don't, there's a good chance that sooner or later something will happen to the PC—loss, theft, virus infection, hard drive crash, natural disaster—and all of your data, much of it irreplaceable, could be gone forever.

Although almost everyone knows that backing up is important, not everyone takes the time and effort to actually do it. That's partly because people tend to discount the possibility of bad things happening, but it's also because in the past, backing up has often required a fair amount of time and effort.

But that's not the case anymore.

These days there are ways to back up data on a Windows PC that are quick, easy, and free, or very nearly so. In this chapter, we'll explore several options, including Windows' built-in File History, System Image, and Backup and Restore features. We'll also discuss third-party services that back up your data online.

## File History

File History is a feature built into Windows 8.x and 10 that automatically backs up any files you store within Documents, Music, Pictures, Video, and Desktop, as well as your Contacts and (Internet Explorer) Favorites. If your PC has copies of files stored on OneDrive, Microsoft's cloud storage service, File History will back them up, too. File History works with an external storage device such as a USB hard drive or flash drive, but it can also back up to a network location such as a home or office server. (We'll assume use of an external drive for this chapter as that's what readers are more likely to have.)

---

File History can only back up files found in the specific folders noted here, so be sure that you store any important files that you want to protect in one of those locations.

---

What's particularly handy about File History is that it doesn't simply store the most recent version of a given file. As the name implies, File History stores multiple versions of each file, which means that it isn't only useful when a file gets wiped out; it can also come to the rescue if you accidentally change a file and then want to go back to a previous version.

Depending on the size and number of files that you have and the capacity of your storage device, File History can retain versions of files going back days, weeks, months, or even years. If you want to keep older versions of files around for as long as possible, you should use as large an external storage device for File History as you can. A good rule of thumb is to use a File History drive that's at least twice the size of your PC's internal storage; for example, if the PC has 1 TB, use a 2 TB drive for File History.

---

Although it's preferred that you use an external drive that's dedicated to File History, it's not required. So, in a pinch, you can use any existing drive with adequate free space as a File History drive. If you want to switch to a new File History drive later, Windows will give you the option to copy File History data from the old drive to the new one.

---

## Backing Up Files

To set up File History, first connect the external drive that you want to use. Windows will ask you to choose what you want to do with the drive, and one of the options that it will offer is Configure this drive for backup via File History (Figure 11-1).

*Figure 11-1. Choose Configure this drive for backup to use it with File History*

What we're about to describe is the process to set up File History on Windows 8.1. Things are slightly different in Windows 10. For example, after you've inserted a drive and opted to use it for File History, Windows 10 will still ask you to choose the drive that you want to use, then automatically turn on File History for that drive. Also, some of the configuration windows look different than the ones shown here. But, overall, File History works the same way in both versions of Windows.

Tap or click this option, then tap or click the File History slider from Off to On and Windows will immediately start copying your data over to the File History drive. This can take a while the first time you turn File History on, but sooner or later the process will complete and Windows will inform you that your files have been backed up as of a certain day and time, as shown in Figure 11-2.

*Figure 11-2.* *Turn on File History and let Windows do the rest*

If you connect a drive and for some reason Windows doesn't ask you what to do with it, just search for and run File History and point it to the drive that you just connected.

For obvious reasons, ideally you'll want to keep your external drive constantly connected so that File History can perform its backups. But what about situations when this isn't practical, for example, when you're using a portable PC such as a notebook or a tablet? File History still works in these scenarios, albeit a bit differently.

When File History's external drive isn't available, files are backed up to a reserved area of the PC hard drive known as the offline cache. File backups stored in the offline cache are automatically copied to the external hard drive the next time the drive is connected.

Although the offline cache ensures that your files get backed up even when the external drive isn't connected, the cache is vulnerable to loss because it's stored on the same hard drive as your original files. To minimize the risk of losing both your files and your most recent backups of those files, you should be sure to connect the File History external drive to your PC regularly—preferably daily. A side benefit is that the more often you connect it, the less time it will take to synchronize the contents with the offline cache.

File History has0020several default options with regard to the size of the offline cache (5% of disk space), how often it saves copies of your files (every hour), and how long it keeps the saved copies (forever). These settings make sense for most people, but if you want to change any of them (for example, save copies of files every 10 or 15 minutes, or keep saved files for only a month or a year), search for and run File History, then choose Advanced Settings to make your changes (Figure 11-3).

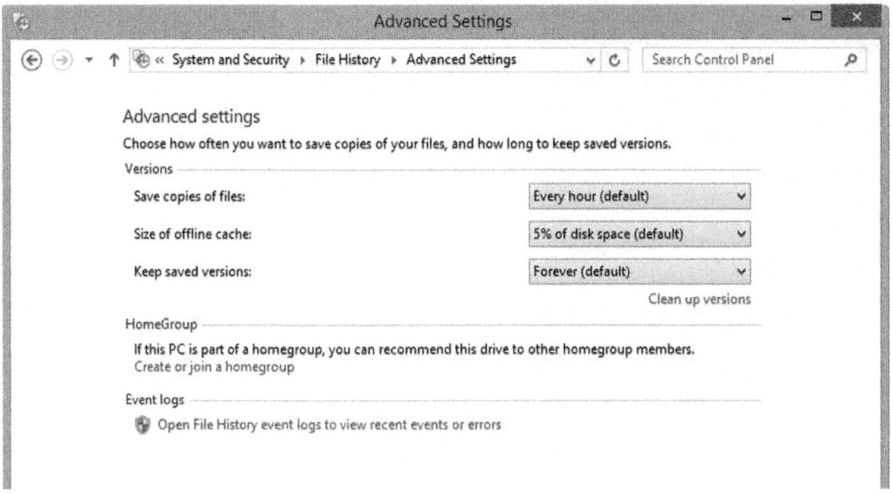

*Figure 11-3.* *File History lets you control settings including how often it saves files and how long it keeps them*

File History works on a per-user basis, so if a PC is shared by multiple people, each user must log in with their own account and turn on File History to protect their own files. A single File History drive can be shared between multiple users of a single PC, multiple computers, or multiple computers on a network. (Connecting a storage device to a home router makes this especially convenient.) (For more on sharing via a network, see Chapter 10.)

# Restoring Files

If you ever find yourself needing a backed-up file (or *all* of your backed-up files), make sure that the File History drive is connected, search for Restore, then choose Restore your files with File History (Figure 11-4).

*Figure 11-4.* *To recover one or more files from backup, choose Restore your files with File History*

The next window that appears will display the most recent backup in File History. That's probably what you are most interested in if you're recovering from a catastrophic problem that wiped out all of your files. In that case, restoring them couldn't be more straightforward—tap or click to highlight each of the icons shown, then click the green Restore button and your files will be copied back to their original locations (Figure 11-5).

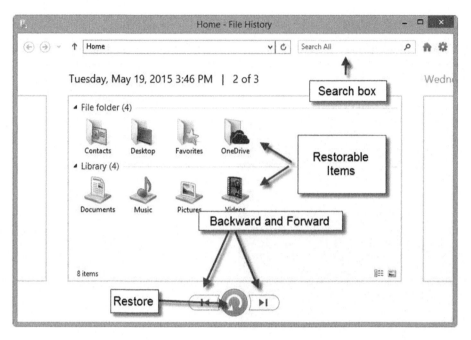

***Figure 11-5.*** *File History's restore window*

If your restore needs to be a bit more selective—say, you want to restore a particular document to the version from a week earlier—tap or click the left arrow to go back to the appropriate day and time, double-tap or click open up Documents, highlight the file you want, then tap or click Restore.

---

An even more straightforward way to browse previous versions of a file—assuming that you haven't deleted it—is to locate the file in File Explorer, select the Home tab (if you're not already in there by default), and then click the History icon in the Ribbon bar.

---

Need a particular file but not exactly sure what it's called or where it's located? Use the search box near the top right of the window. If searching turns up the file you were looking for, right-click (or tap and hold) the file and select Restore.

Incidentally, you don't need to rely on file names to determine whether or not a given file actually contains the information that you think it does. Right click or long tap a file and select Preview to view its contents so you know for sure. (To preview a file when you're viewing it in search results, double-click or tap it.)

There may be situations in which you want to restore files to a different location rather than to their original location. In these cases, highlight the items that you want to restore, but don't use the green Restore button. Instead, right click or tap and hold your highlighted items and select "Restore to" to specify a new location.

Finally, if you do try to restore a file to a location where a file with the same name already exists, Windows will ask you whether you want to copy the new file over the existing one, skip the file, or compare info (time, date, and size) for the files before deciding (Figure 11-6).

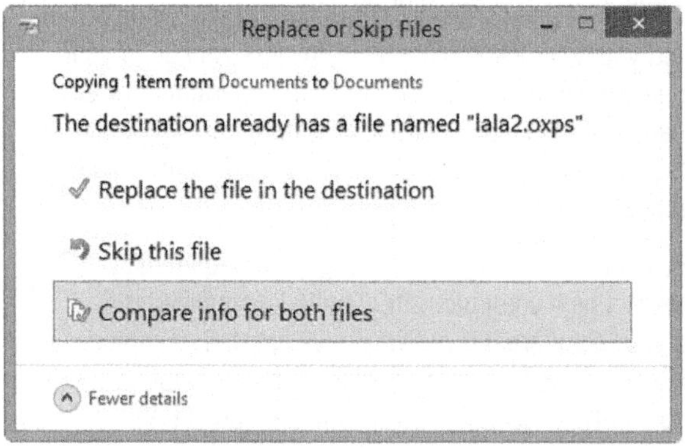

**Replace or Skip Files** — □ ×

Copying 1 item from Documents to Documents

The destination already has a file named "lala2.oxps"

✓ Replace the file in the destination

↪ Skip this file

⎘ Compare info for both files

⌃ Fewer details

*Figure 11-6. Your options in the event of a file conflict during a restore*

## SYSTEM IMAGE

There's another kind of backup built into Windows, called System Image. It's a holdover from earlier versions of Windows, and Microsoft has hidden it to deemphasize it relative to File History (e.g., searching for "system image" won't produce any results). Nevertheless, it's still accessible via a link in the lower right corner of the File History window, as shown in Figure 11-7.

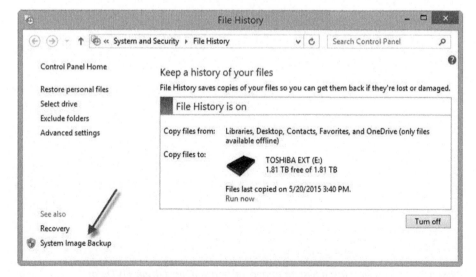

*Figure 11-7. System Image Backup is buried in the corner of File History*

131

Unlike File History, System Image doesn't just backup the personal files you store in a handful of locations. It backs up the entire contents of your PC—everything from files to applications to operating system and settings. But it doesn't let you choose what to backup—with System Image, it's everything or nothing.

On the plus side, this means that you have a complete soup-to-nuts backup of your PC that you can restore in one step without having to reinstall the operating system, then applications, and then, finally, your files. By contrast, a System Image Backup is obsolete the moment you create it because it won't reflect any of the subsequent changes you make to your personal data.

Although a System Image Backup isn't especially helpful for file management, it can be worthwhile to make one on a new computer after you've customized the operating system and installed your software but *before* you've created or copied any personal data to it. You can save a System Image Backup to an external hard disk, to one or more DVDs, or to a network location, as shown in Figure 11-8.

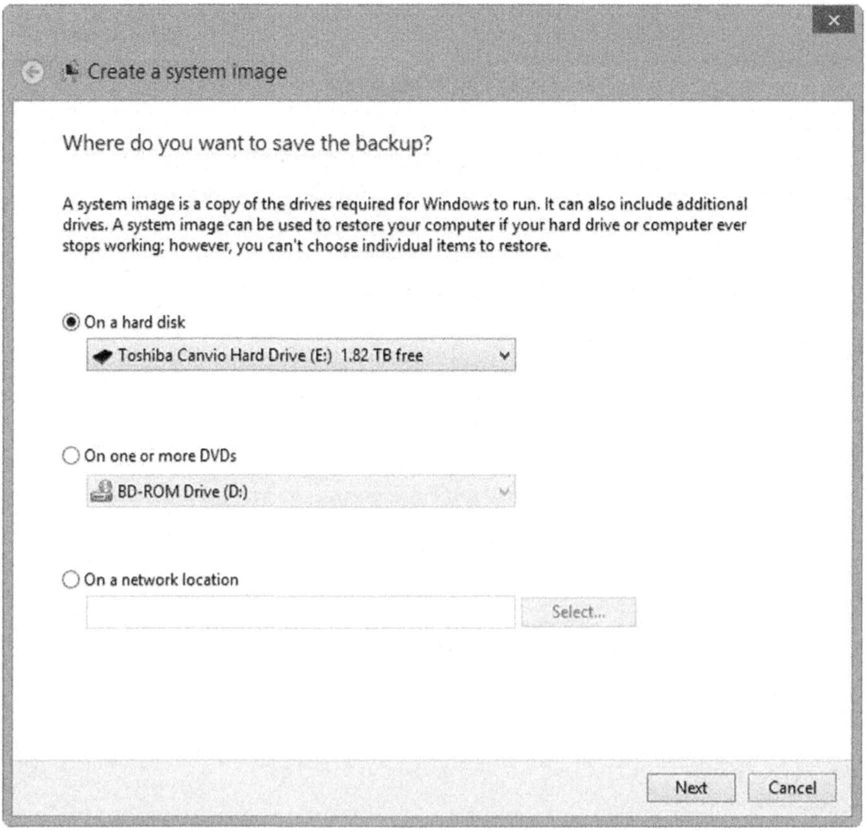

*Figure 11-8.* *You can save a System Image Backup to a hard drive, DVDs, or network location*

For more information on how to use System Image Backup, see windows.microsoft.
com/en-us/windows/back-up-programs-system-settings-files#1TC=windows-7.

# Backup and Restore

Speaking of stuff from older versions of Windows, once upon a time Windows included a built-in backup program called Backup and Restore. It came with Windows Vista and Windows 7, and although Microsoft removed it from the operating system beginning with Windows 8, the company brought it back for Windows 10.

In most repects, File History is far superior to Backup and Restore. It's easier to use, and it backs up your files continuously, wheras Backup and Restore can't do it more often than once a day.

So why are we even mentioning it here? Other than the fact that Microsoft saw fit to bring it back to life in its newest version of Windows, Backup and Restore can do one thing that File History can't, and that's back up folders that you specify, not just the standard folders (Documents, Pictures, etc.).

Although we think it makes a lot more sense to consolidate all of your data within the standard folders and protect them via File History, if you have Windows 10 and you want the option to back up folders of your own choosing, have at it. (If you're still using Windows 7, Backup and Restore might be a good way to get your files over to a new Windows 10 PC.) To find Backup and Restore in Windows 10, search for Backup and Restore (Windows 7). For more information on Backup and Restore see windows. microsoft.com/en-us/windows7/products/features/backup-and-restore. (Although this link references Windows 7, the Backup and Restore feature works pretty much the same way in Windows 10.)

# Online Backup

Having your files backed up to an external hard drive will save your bacon in most situations, including a hard drive failure, virus infection, loss or theft of a laptop, or accidentally deleting a file. But there are some scenarios in which that external drive may not help you because it succumbed to the same fate as the PC it is backing up.

One example is if your home was burglarized and the thief makes off with both your PC and the backup drive that was connected to it. Others include a catastrophic event that could potential wipe out everything, such as a fire, flood, tornado or hurricane, and so on. Suffice it to say that having your files backed up solely on an external hard drive doesn't guarantee that you won't lose all of your valuable data under certain circumstances.

To protect yourself against the unexpected loss of a backup, it's strongly recommended that you also use some form of online (a.k.a. cloud-based) backup. Numerous companies provide this type of service, which use your Internet connection to continuously upload backup copies of your files to their servers for safekeeping. These services work much the same way as File History except that your "backup drive" safely resides hundreds or thousands of miles away in a data center.

Prices for online backup services can vary based depending on the provider and the features desired, but costs generally start at around $60 for an annual subscription.

Although online backup has some definite advantages over backing up to a directly connected hard drive (this is often referred to as *local* backup), there are a couple of downsides to be aware of as well.

- *It can be slow.* Compared to the speed of the connection between a PC and a USB hard drive, backing up via your Internet connection can be quite sluggish. This means doing an initial backup of a PC with lots of data on it can take an extremely long time—many hours, days, or even weeks, depending on how much data you have and the speed of your connection (and you'll need to remain connected the entire time that the backup is in progress).

  Similarly, if you ever needed to do a complete restore of your data, getting it all back down to your PC can be extremely time-consuming. That said, once an initial backup is complete, subsequent backups generally take just seconds or minutes because only new or changed files need to be uploaded.

- *It can get pricey.* Many online backup providers charge a premium unless you pay for their services one or more years in advance, as well as charge extra for more than a certain amount of space, to back up multiple computers, to back up very large files (such as videos), or for certain convenience features, such as the ability to back up both online and to your own hard drive (to avoid the slow restore problem described earlier).

## It's Worth It Though

Caveats aside, given that the value of your personal files can be incalculable, backing up online can be a good substitute for, or complement to, having a local backup. Here are a few of our favorite online backup services:

Carbonite

`http://www.carbonite.com/online-backup/personal/how-it-works`

CrashPlan

`https://www.code42.com/crashplan/`

Mozy

`http://mozy.com/product/mozy/personal`

# CHAPTER 12

■ ■ ■

# Keeping Your Personal Data Secure via Encryption

There's a pretty good chance that your computer contains all sorts of personal or sensitive information—legal, financial, or medical documents, —and so on—that you wouldn't want a stranger to get their hands on.

You may think that your Windows account password protects your sensitive files from prying eyes, and it does, but only up to a certain point. Although keeping your Windows password secret (it is a secret, right?) will prevent anyone from logging into your account to view your files, there are ways to access a PC's storage without going through Windows.

One way is to use a so-called Live CD or DVD, which contains an operating system (typically a version of Linux) that runs entirely in the PC's memory (RAM). Starting a PC with a Live CD/DVD allows someone to bypass Windows and use another operating system to access the hard drive without making any permanent changes to it (i.e., you don't have to "install" the operating system on the hard drive). Another method is to simply remove the hard drive from a PC and connect it to different computer in order to directly access the contents while circumventing any restrictions Windows may have put on files or folders.

If your PC should ever be lost or stolen, these methods will be among the first things someone of malicious intent will do in order to mine the computer for exploitable information. But you can keep your data secure in this kind of scenario by encrypting it.

## What Is Encryption?

Simply put, encrypting data means scrambling it with a special algorithm and a secret code called an encryption key. Once data is scrambled in this way it becomes gibberish, so the only way to convert it back into its original, readable form is with that encryption key.

Encryption comes in many different forms. Beyond the various encryption algorithms that exist, there are numerous ways to implement encryption. For example, some kinds of encryption are built into Windows, but you can also get it via third-party hardware or software. Some encryption products are designed to encrypt specific files (or the folders containing them), whereas others encrypt an entire storage device, including the operating system and applications. (We'll discuss examples of the latter in this chapter.)

---

## HOW WELL DOES ENCRYPTION PROTECT YOUR DATA?

Unfortunately, there's no easy answer to that question. No form of security is 100 percent effective, and it's an axiom that virtually any form of security can be defeated given enough time, money, and effort. It's also important to remember that security and convenience reside on opposite ends of a continuum. That is, when security goes up, convenience goes down, and vice versa. Some forms of encryption can be quite onerous, requiring a lot of time and effort to use. The methods we'll discuss here are designed to be transparent—that is, once they're turned on, they more or less work automatically, and in the background, without significantly impacting how you use the computer.

---

# Windows Device Encryption

One of the easiest ways to protect your data on a Windows 8.1 or Windows 10 PC is via the built-in Device Encryption feature. Device Encryption automatically encrypts the entire contents of your computer. But there's a catch—using Windows' Device Encryption feature requires a PC to support a technology called InstantGo, which among other things, means that the PC contains a built-in Trusted Platform Module (TPM), which is a special security chip that can store encryption keys.

In addition, to use Device Encryption you must log into Windows using a Microsoft account (which links you to Microsoft's various online services) with administrator permissions, rather than a Local account.

---

For more on the differences between a Microsoft account and a Local account, see Chapter 4.

---

If your PC is a modern tablet, laptop, or convertible/hybrid type system (the kind that can function as either a laptop or a tablet) and came with Windows 8.1 preinstalled (i.e., it wasn't upgraded from a previous version of Windows), it might support Device Encryption. (Windows desktops are unlikely to support it, however.)

Assuming that your PC meets the hardware requirements and that you're currently using your Microsoft account to log into Windows, Device Encryption may even already be running. In any event, the easiest way to know for sure whether or not your Windows PC supports/is using Device Encryption is to check for it.

Search for "encrypt" and look for *Change device encryption settings,* as shown in Figure 12-1.

***Figure 12-1.*** *If you see this setting, your PC supports the Windows Device Encryption feature*

---

If you don't see Change device encryption settings, your PC doesn't support Device Encryption.

---

Depending on whether device encryption is already running or not, you'll see a button labeled either Turn off or Turn on (Figure 12-2). If you find the former, device encryption is already running and you're good to go. If you see the latter, just tap or click the button, and Windows will automatically begin encrypting the system. You can keep using it while this happens. (You may be asked to confirm information about your Microsoft account before you can activate device encryption.)

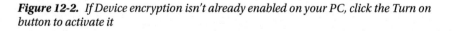

## Device encryption

Device encryption helps protect your files and folders from unauthorized access in case your device is lost or stolen.

Device encryption is off.

Turn on

***Figure 12-2.*** *If Device encryption isn't already enabled on your PC, click the Turn on button to activate it*

During the encryption process, a recovery key will automatically be uploaded to your Microsoft account. You don't need to make a record of the recovery key, as it will be associated with and available through your Microsoft account.

137

## WHY DOES DEVICE ENCRYPTION REQUIRE A MICROSOFT ACCOUNT?

Device encryption requires a Microsoft account mainly for convenience, because it eliminates the need for you to keep track of your own recovery key. Storing the recovery key online within your Micosoft account is the best way to ensure that it will be accessible to you when you need it, because even if you forget your Microsoft account password, Microsoft has other ways to verify that you are you (such as by sending a numeric code to your mobile phone). Without the Microsoft account you'd have to record your own recovery key, and if you were to somehow lose or forget it, there would be no way to recover your encrypted data.

That said, if you'd also prefer to save your own copy of the recovery key, go to windows.microsoft.com/recoverykey and sign in with your Microsoft account info. There you'll be able to view, print, or copy and paste your 56-digit recovery key. Note that it will be referred to as a "BitLocker" recovery key; device encryption actually uses a Microsoft encryption technology called BitLocker, which is a good segue to talk about it.

# BitLocker

Windows Device Encryption is actually based on a predecessor encryption technology from Microsoft called BitLocker. Although using BitLocker isn't quite as effortless as using Device Encryption, it accomplishes much the same thing—it encrypts the contents of your hard drive to thwart any attempt to bypass Windows and directly access your files.

But, as with Device Encryption, BitLocker comes with a catch—it's only available on the Pro and Enterprise editions of Windows 8 or Windows 10, which are business-oriented versions of Windows, which include features not found in the "regular" consumer-oriented Windows editions.

Fortunately, it's easy enough to determine whether or not you have a version of Windows that includes BitLocker: just search for "bitlocker". If you see a result called Manage Bitlocker, as shown in Figure 12-3, then you've got it; if not, you don't.

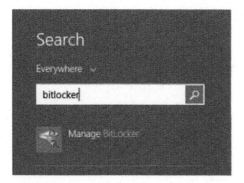

***Figure 12-3.*** *If you don't see Manage BitLocker when searching, your version of Windows lacks the feature*

## GET BITLOCKER WITH THE WINDOWS 8.1 PRO PACK

If you didn't find BitLocker on your system, you can get it (along with other new features) by upgrading your system via the Windows 8.1 Pro Pack. It's not exactly cheap—the Pro Pack costs $100 if you buy it online directly from Microsoft, although you can often find it cheaper from other online retailers such as Amazon.

Price aside, however, adding the Pro Pack is an easy upgrade because there is nothing to download or install—you're actually buying a product key, which is an alphanumeric code that you enter into your computer to instantly unlock the higher version of Windows without disturbing any of your existing software or data.

To buy an upgrade code (or use one you've previously purchased), search for "add features", then tap or click Add Features to Windows 8.1, then follow the prompts as shown in Figure 12-4 to obtain or enter a code.

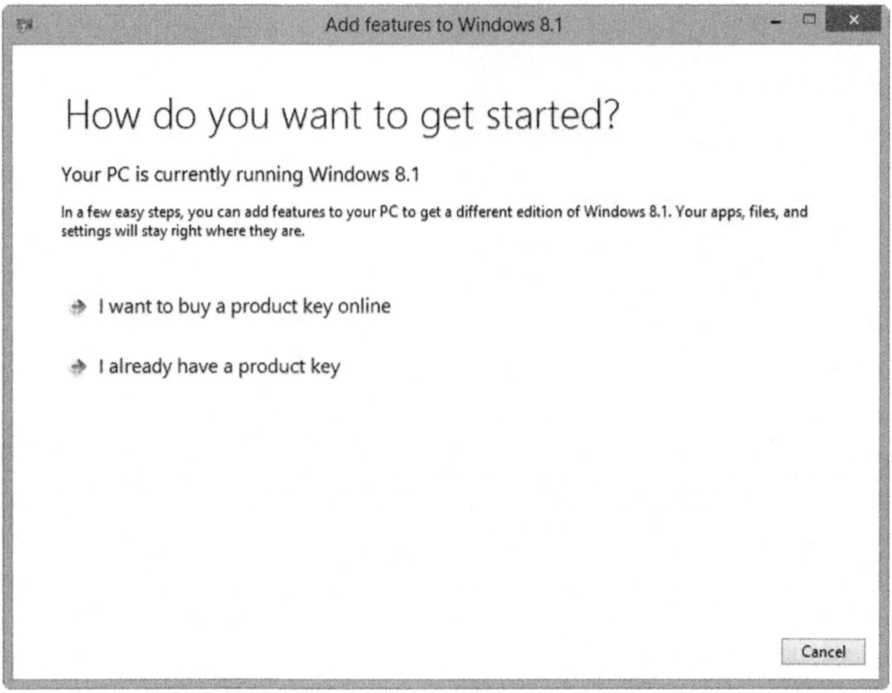

**Figure 12-4.** *If you want BitLocker but don't have Windows 8.1 Pro, you can buy a product key to upgrade*

Got Windows 10? As with Windows 8.1 you'll need the Pro version of Windows 10 in order to use BitLocker. Microsoft will likely offer Windows 10 users an upgrade similar to that for Windows 8.1, but the company hadn't announced its plans at the time that we wrote this book.

# Using BitLocker

Once you've run BitLocker, there's a good chance that you're going to see the window shown in Figure 12-5. As we mentioned earlier, a TPM is a special security chip that's built into certain laptops, but many models lack one. Eventually, all laptops will likely have TPMs, but as of this writing they're far more common in business-oriented computers than consumer-oriented models.

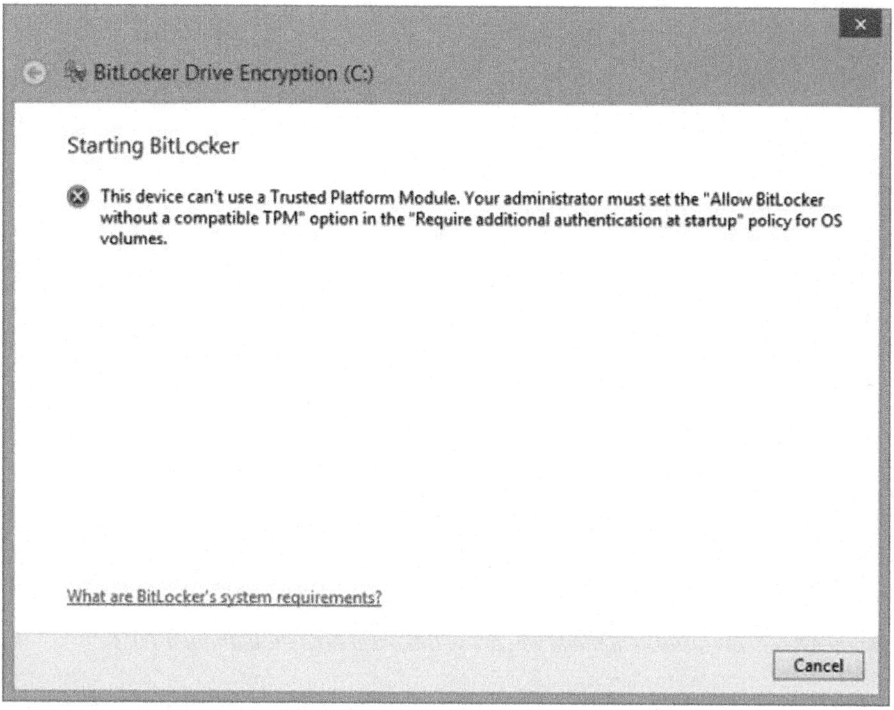

*Figure 12-5.* *If you see this )window after attempting to turn on BitLocker, it means that your computer lacks a TPM chip*

Although lacking a TPM chip is a showstopper if you want to use the Device Encryption that we discussed in the previous section, you can still use BitLocker even if you don't have a TPM—you just need to make a system tweak first.

---

If your PC was provided by your company and is under control of a network administrator, you may not be able to perform the following tweak.

---

To allow BitLocker to run on a system without a TPM, go to the Start screen and search for gpedit (or edit group policy) to launch the Local Group Policy Editor. Then navigate to Computer Configuration|Administrative Templates|Windows Components|BitLocker Drive Encryption|Operating System Drives. Finally, double-click Require additional authentication at startup, click enabled, and make sure *Allow BitLocker without a compatible TPM* is checked (Figure 12-6). Click Apply, then OK, then rerun BitLocker.

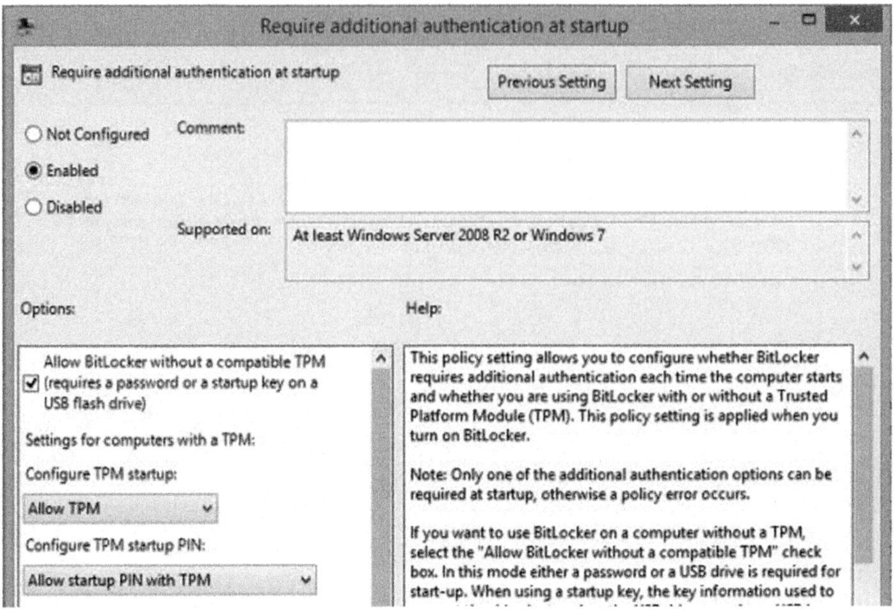

*Figure 12-6. This tweak will allow you to use BitLocker on a PC without a TPM*

Once you've got BitLocker running, you'll see the window shown in Figure 12-7. Click **Turn on BitLocker** next to the hard drive that you want to protect. (If your computer happens to have multiple hard drives, you'll see a link for each one, as BitLocker must be turned on separately for each drive.)

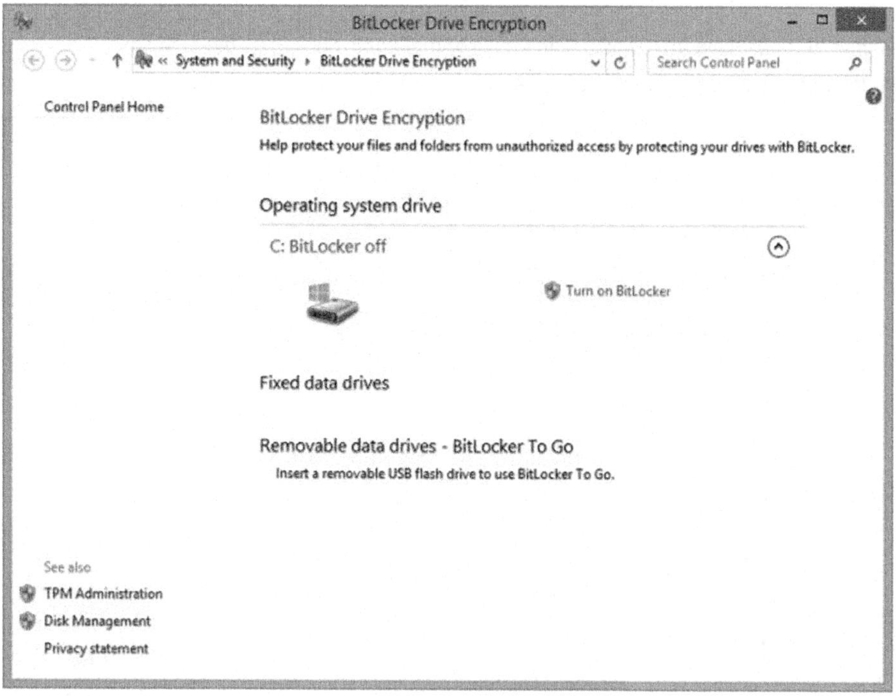

*Figure 12-7.* *Click Turn on BitLocker next to a drive to encrypt it*

Next you'll be asked how you want to unlock your drive at startup (i.e., each time you turn on your PC). Your options are to insert a USB Flash drive or enter a password (Figure 12-8).

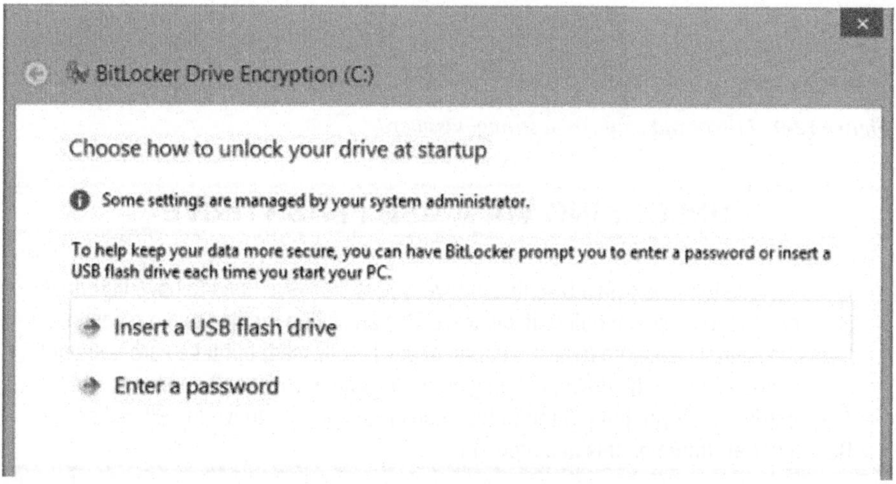

*Figure 12-8.* *You can unlock your PC at startup with either a USB flash drive or a password*

143

If your PC does have a TPM, you won't have to make this choice, as the TPM will automatically unlock your drive at startup.

For this example, we'll opt for using a password. Enter and confirm your password, and be sure it's a strong one. Click the link provided for more information.

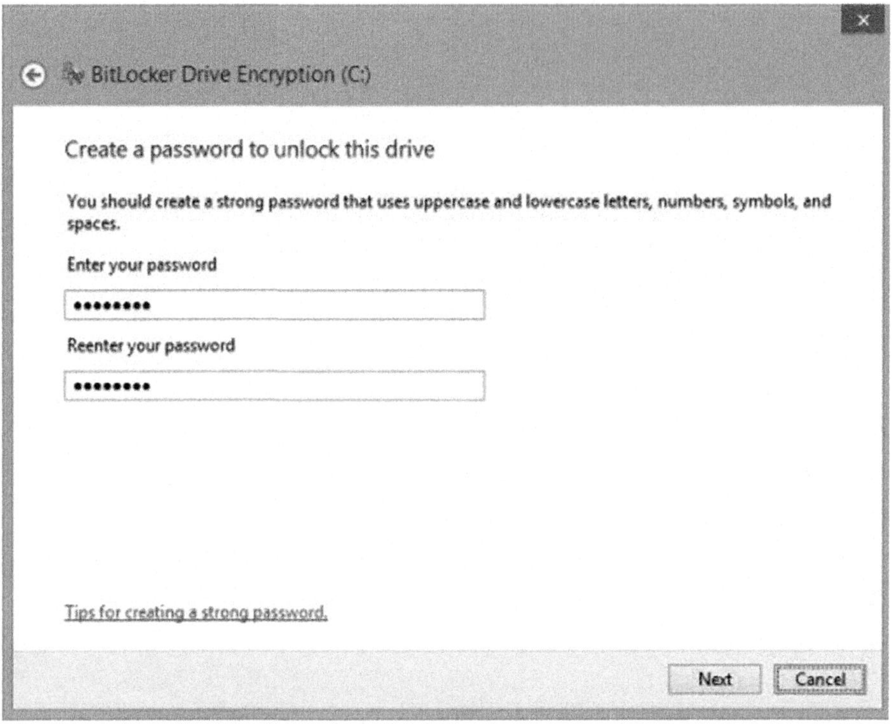

**Figure 12-9.** *Enter (and confirm) a strong password*

## UNLOCKING VIA A USB FLASH DRIVE

If you choose to unlock via a USB Flash drive, you will always need to have that drive inserted into your system before it will start. This unlocking method is more secure than choosing a password (which can potentially be guessed) but take care—should you misplace or lose the drive (and they are quite small), you won't be able to use the computer until you jump through the hoops required to retrieve the BitLocker Recovery Key. (more on this in a moment).

Next, Bitlocker will ask you how you want to back up your recovery key (Figure 12-10). Your options are to Save to your Microsoft account, a USB flash drive, a file, or to print it. You can—and should—choose multiple backup methods so that you have a fallback in case one is unavailable. Choose your backup methods one at a time, follow the steps, and then click Next when you're done.

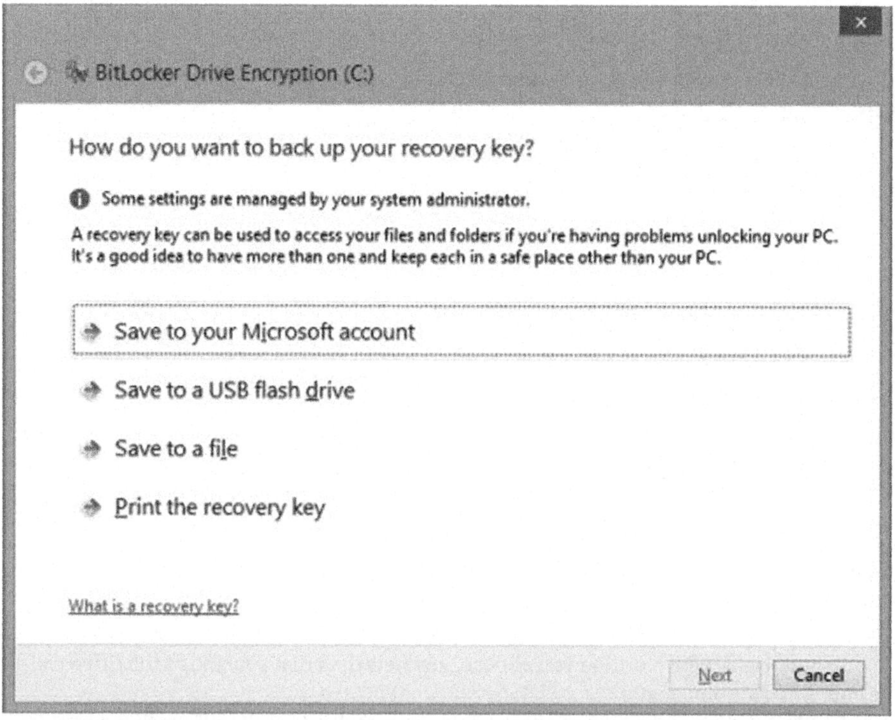

**Figure 12-10.** *You must back up your recovery key via at least one (and preferably more than one) of these methods*

---

Save to a file will only work if your PC has multiple internal storage devices; you can't save the recovery key to the drive you're encrypting.

---

Now it's time to decide how much of the drive to encrypt (Figure 12-11). If you're doing this on a brand new computer, the default option, Encrypt used disk space only, will get the job done faster, but if the computer's been in use for a while already, the Encrypt entire drive option will ensure that free space, which likely contains previously deleted data, is also encrypted.

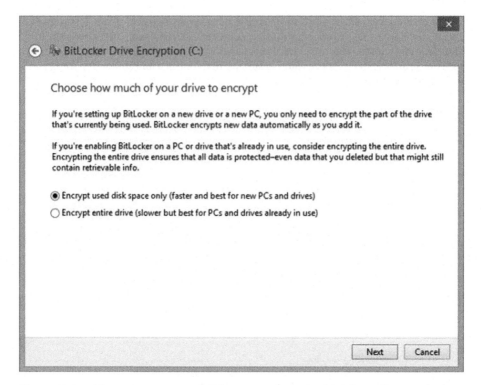

*Figure 12-11. Choose to encrypt used disk space or the entire drive depending on whether or not your PC is new*

Regardless of which option you choose, any new data that you add to the drive will be encrypted automatically.

Finally, you'll be asked if you are ready to encrypt the drive. You'll see that a box labeled Run BitLocker system check is checked (Figure 12-12). It's strongly recommended that you keep the box checked, as BitLocker will test to make sure that your unlock password or key is working correctly before your drive is encrypted. Click Continue. At this point, you'll need to restart your computer to initiate the encryption process.

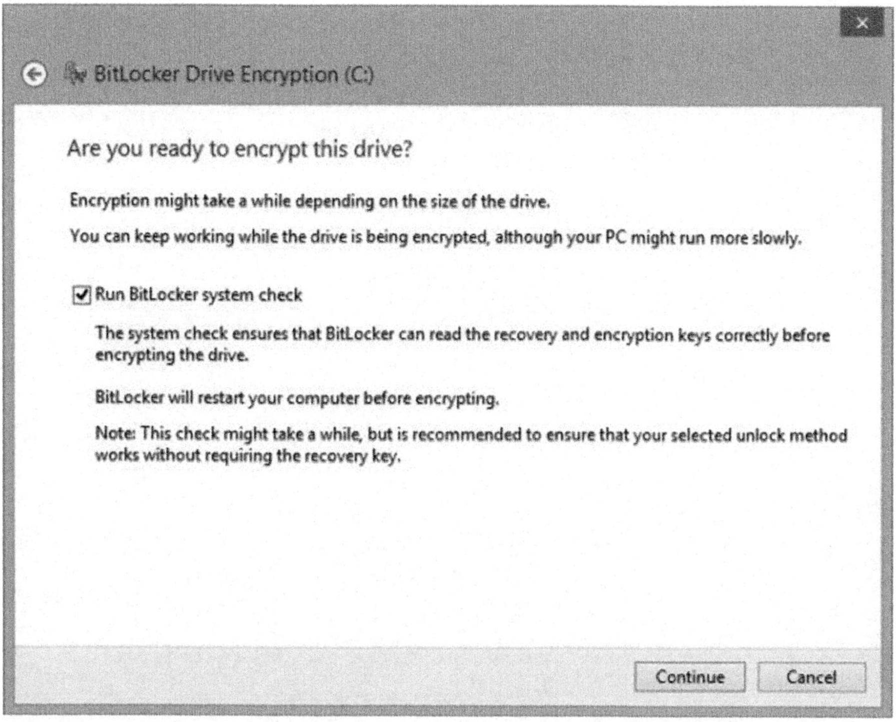

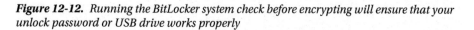

*Figure 12-12. Running the BitLocker system check before encrypting will ensure that your unlock password or USB drive works properly*

When your system restarts, you'll be prompted to provide the Bitlocker unlock password (Figure 12-13) or insert the USB drive you created. (Note the option to press ESC for BitLocker recovery; select this should you ever forget your unlock password or lose the USB drive.) Once you've entered the unlock password, Windows will finish loading and start encrypting your drive. You can use the computer while it's being encrypted, but be patient because the process can take many hours to complete and performance may be quite sluggish until it does.

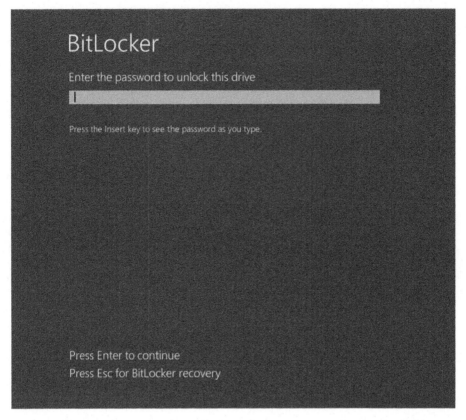

*Figure 12-13.* *Enter your unlock password (or USB key) to make sure that it works. (Going forward, you'll also need to do this each time you start your BitLocker-encrypted PC.)*

# Using BitLocker on Removable Drives

Maybe the files you want to protect aren't on your PC but, rather, on a removable storage device such as a USB hard drive or Flash drive. If so, you can use BitLocker to encrypt those drives, too—just connect the drive that you want to encrypt, locate it in File Explorer, right click it, and select Turn on BitLocker (Figure 12-14). You'll go through steps similar to those outlined earlier—choosing and confirming a password, backing up a recovery key, and so on—and when you're done the drive will begin encrypting. Don't remove the drive during encryption. If you absolutely must, click Pause to put encryption on hold before doing so.

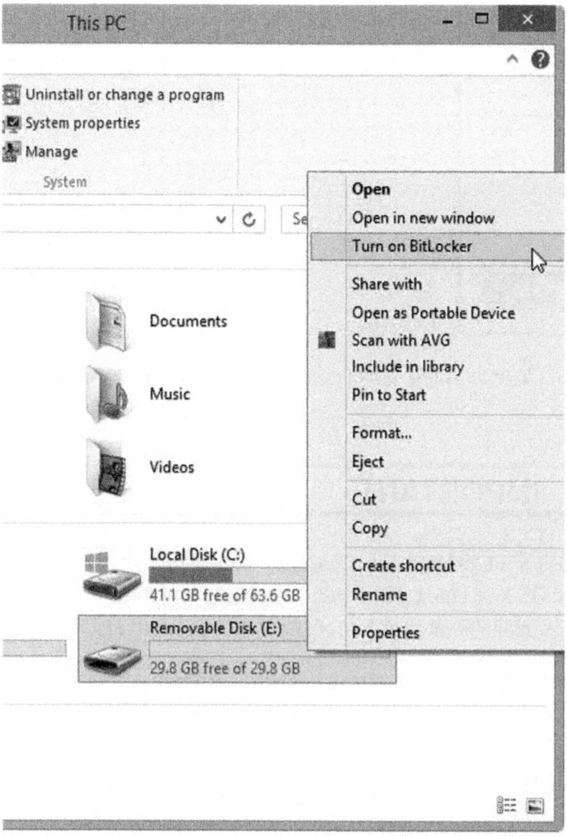

***Figure 12-14.*** *Right click a removable drive and choose Turn on BitLocker to encrypt it.(Note the lock icon for drive C:, indicating that this drive is also protected by BitLocker.)*

Once a removable drive is encrypted, you'll need to enter the unlock password each time you insert the drive into a Windows 10, Windows 8.x, or Windows 7 computer (Figure 12-15).

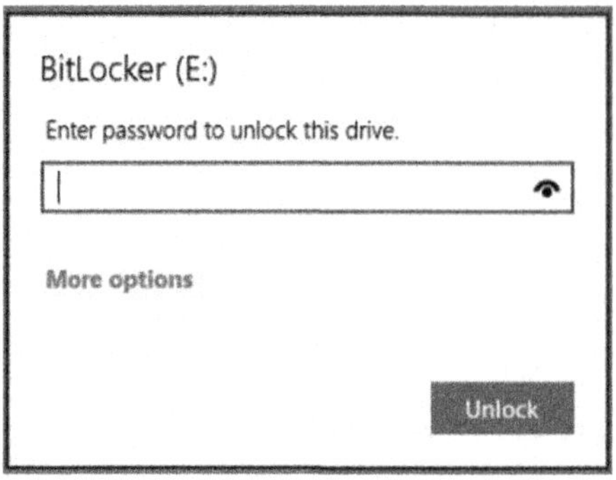

**Figure 12-15.** *Insert a BitLocker to Go–encrypted drive; you'll have to enter a password before you can access it*

---

## IMPORTANT

There is no official way to access a BitLocker to Go drive from non-Windows operating systems such as Mac OS X or Linux, but a free third-party tool that purports to make this possible is available at `www.hsc.fr/ressources/outils/dislocker`.

---

# Other Encryption Options

If your PC doesn't support Device Encryption and you don't have a version of Windows that includes BitLocker, there are third-party software options available. For a no-cost option, look into either VeraCrypt (veracrypt.codeplex.com) or CipherShed (ciphershed. org), both of which are based on the same code as TrueCrypt, which was arguably the most popular third-party encryption software until it was abruptly discontinued in May 2014. Both VeraCrypt and CipherShed can encrypt internal and removable drives, and both are compatible with Windows, Mac OS X, or Linux (although neither is quite as user-friendly as BitLocker).

If your main concern is carrying encrypting data with you on a removable drive, you should also consider hardware-encrypted USB hard drives and flash drives. These drives contain a built-in security chip, so they provide very strong, fast, encryption that works on any computer, regardless of operating system used. They also integrate a numeric keypad (Figure 12-16) or biometric scanner so you can access them via a PIN code or swipe of your finger. Two companies that make these types of drives are Apricorn (`www.apricorn.com`) and IronKey (`www.ironkey.com`). But be forewarned—these drives can be up to ten times the price of ordinary drives with the same storage capacity.

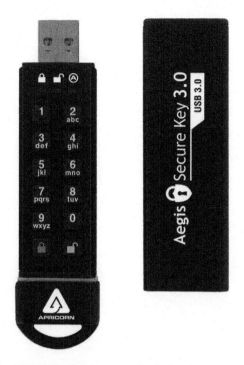

***Figure 12-16.*** *An example of a hardware-encrypted USB flash drive with integrated keypad*

# CHAPTER 13

■ ■ ■

# Transfer Your Files to a New PC

If you're like many people, you might be inclined to buy a new PC every few years in order to benefit from the latest in performance and features. But when you've spent years accumulating thousands of personal data files on an existing PC, the thought of transferring all that stuff over to a new computer can seem like a daunting task. Talk about a file management chore!

Fortunately, it doesn't necessarily have to be a chore. There are ways to automatically transfer all of your valued files from one PC to another—if not always quickly (data transfers can take time, especially when you have a lot of it), then at least reliably and thoroughly.

Windows includes several built-in data transfer features, including File History, Windows Easy Transfer, and Backup and Restore. But because the presence and capabilities of these features aren't necessarily consistent between successive versions of Windows, the version of Windows that's running on both your old and new PCs will determine the transfer method that makes the most sense. Other potential ways to transfer files between PCs include synching them to the same cloud storage service or using one of the available third-party tools to do the job.

## LAPLINK PC MOVER EXPRESS

As this book was being completed, Microsoft announced that it was making Laplink's PC Mover Express software available as a free download for a limited time. The software can transfer files and folders from a system running an old Windows PC to a new one, but it's only available until August 31, 2016. For more information on Laplink PC Mover Express or to download the software, see `www.microsoft.com/en-us/windows/transfer-your-data`.

Before we get into the details for each of these transfer methods, Table 13-1 shows when you'll want to use the built-in Windows features.

***Table 13-1.*** *The transfer method to use will depend on which version of Windows is running on both your old and new PCs*

| Old PC (From) | New PC (To) | Use |
|---|---|---|
| Windows 8.1, Windows 10 | Windows 8.1, Windows 10 | File History |
| Windows 7, 8 | Windows 8, 8.1 | Windows Easy Transfer |
| Windows 7 | Windows 10 | Backup and Restore |

# File History

If you want to get your files from an existing Windows 8.1 or Windows 10 PC over a new one that's also running either Windows 8.1 or Windows 10, your best bet to do so is via Windows' built-in File History feature.

File History, as you may recall from Chapter 11, automatically backs up files that you've stored on your desktop and any of the standard Windows folders (such as Documents, Music, Pictures, and Videos) to an external storage device, which you can then use to transfer the backed-up files over to your new PC. In a nutshell, if you've been backing up regularly with File History, the job of getting it all to a new PC is already half done.

---

■ **Note** Before proceeding, be sure you've enabled File History on your existing PC as described in Chapter 11 and have completed the initial backup.

---

## Transfer Files Off the Old PC

Before doing the transfer, you'll want to make sure that your File History backup is current. With your old PC's File History drive connected, run File History by searching for it from the Start screen, then click the Run now link (Figure 13-1) to bring your backup up to date with the latest versions of your files. Be sure not to create, modify, or delete any files while you're File History backup is running; otherwise, those changes may not be reflected in the backup.

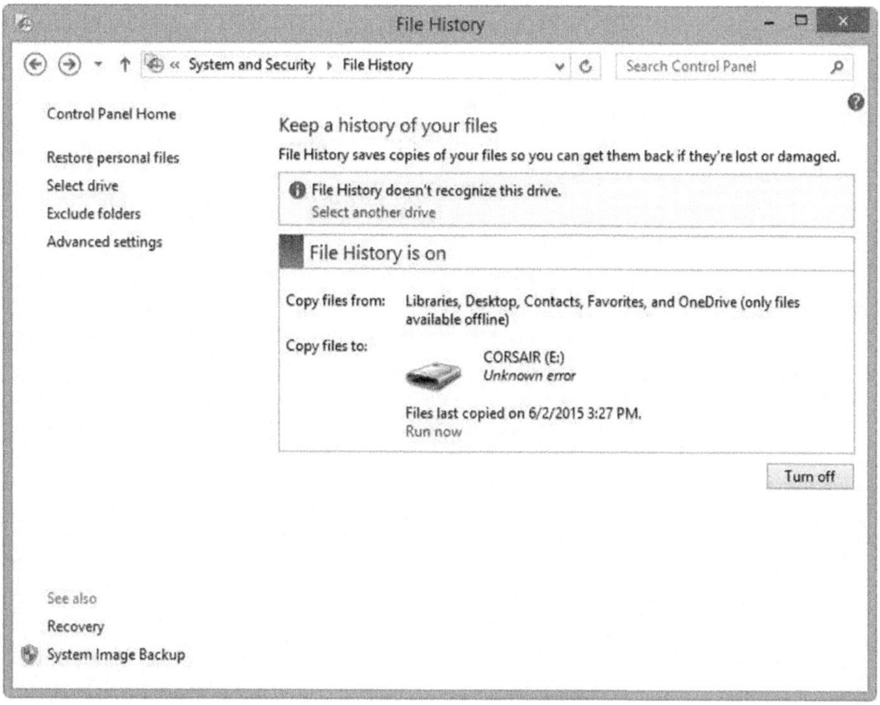

*Figure 13-1.* *Make sure that your File History backup is up to date before restoring it to a new PC*

Once the backup is complete (you'll know it's done when the Run now link reappears), you can disconnect the drive from the PC and connect it to the new PC.

## Transfer Files to the New PC

On the new PC, search for and select "file history". When it opens, choose "Select drive" near the upper left corner of the window. Choose the drive that contains the backup from the old PC and check I want to use a previous backup on this File History drive. Verify the backup that you just updated on the old PC is highlighted below under Select an existing backup and click OK (Figure 13-2). If you see multiple backups listed, choose the one that matches your computer's name and the date/time of its last backup.

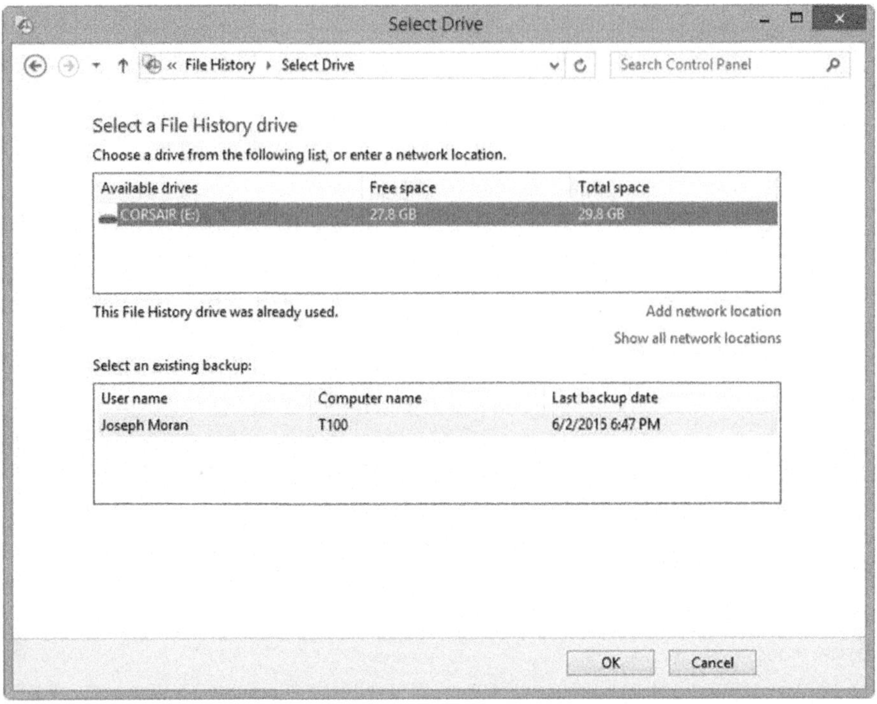

***Figure 13-2.*** *To restore files from an old PC to a new one, specify that you want to use a previous backup from your File History drive*

This should return you to the window shown in Figure 13-1. From there, select Restore personal files and you'll see File History, window which should be familiar from Chapter 11 (Figure 13-3). Because in this case you want to transfer all files from your old PC to your new one, highlight all items from the most recent backup (or press CTRL +A to easily select all items) and then press the green button to begin the transfer. When it's complete, all of the files that used to be on your old PC will be on your new one.

**Figure 13-3.** *Highlight all the items and press the green "restore" button to transfer the files to your new PC*

---

■ **Note**    For more tips on how to make a new PC like your old one, see
windows.microsoft.com/en-us/windows-8/make-new-old-pc.

---

# Windows Easy Transfer

If you want to move your files over to a Windows 8.1 PC from one running Windows 7 or Windows 8, the Windows Easy Transfer feature built into all three operating systems is the way to go.

Windows Easy Transfer is actually somewhat more customizable and comprehensive than File History. When you run Windows Easy Transfer on your old PC it scans the computer for user accounts and data files stored in standard folders such as Documents, Music, Pictures, and Videos for each account that it finds. Windows Easy Transfer automatically tags all of these items for transfer and lets you customize the transfer by selecting additional folders and/or excluding folders that were automatically selected.

Once you're satisfied with the selections, Windows Easy Transfer will copy all the data to an external hard disk or flash drive where it's compressed into a single file to save space. Then, when you connect the hard disk or flash drive to the new PC and open the file, the contents of your old PC are expanded and copied into their corresponding locations on the new computer. If user accounts from the old PC don't yet exist on the new PC, Windows Easy Transfer will create them.

157

# Transfer Files Off the Old PC

To use Windows Easy Transfer, start on the old PC and find Windows Easy Transfer by searching for "easy" from the Start menu. (You must be using an administrator account to run it.)

---

■ **Note**    After you click Next on the initial screen, you'll be given an option to do the transfer via an Easy Transfer cable, a network, or via an external hard disk or USB flash drive. Be sure to choose the external hard disk option because it's the only way that a Windows 8.1 PC can accept the transferred files.

---

On the next screen, select This is my old computer and Windows Easy Transfer will begin analyzing the PC to determine which files should be transferred. Be patient for this step—it may take some time to complete if you have a large number of files.

Once the analysis is complete, you'll see a screen similar to the one in Figure 13-4, which shows the user accounts that have been identified, how much data has been selected for transfer within each one, and at the lower right, next to Easy Transfer file size, the total amount of data to be transferred (so the external drive that you use should have at least this much free space).

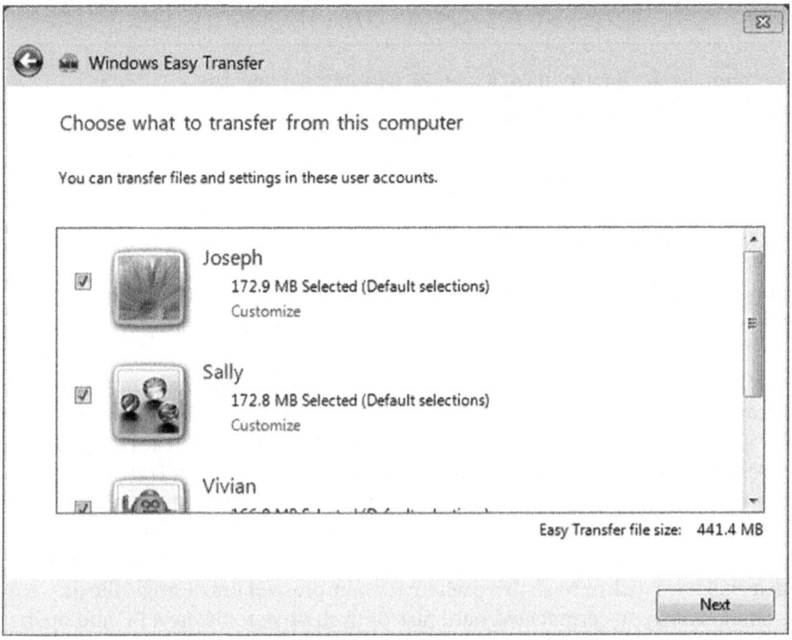

***Figure 13-4.*** *Windows Easy Transfer automatically scans for user accounts and files, then selects what it determines should be transferred to the new PC*

Note that by default Windows Easy Transfer will automatically transfer files for every account on the Windows 7 PC (including the Guest account) as well as the contents of shared "Public" folders. If you don't want to transfer all of that, clear the check mark next to an item. To view or change what will be transferred for a particular account, click Customize under an account name, and a window will appear (Figure 13-5) from which you can uncheck any of the default folders. To add or exclude any other folders on the PC from the transfer, click Advanced (Figure 13-6).

***Figure 13-5.*** *Clicking Customize lets you exclude any of the default folders for a given account*

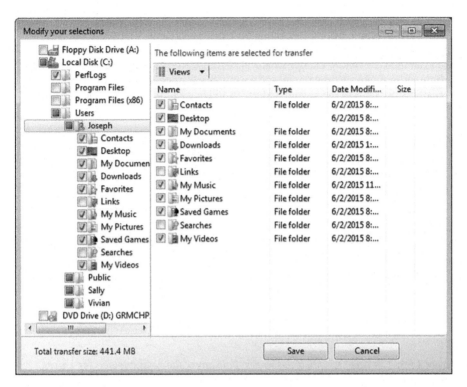

***Figure 13-6.*** *Click Advanced to add or exclude folders from the PC other than the defaults folders for a particular account*

---

■ **Note**    If you click Customize, you may see entries labeled Program Settings and Windows Settings. Be advised that Windows Easy Transfer saves this information but can't transfer it between different versions of Windows. When you initiate the transfer on the new PC, a window will appear informing you that Windows Easy Transfer can only transfer files, not settings.

---

After you customize your selections and click Next, you'll be asked to if you want to protect your Easy Transfer File with a password. **It's strongly recommended that you do so; otherwise, anyone who gets their hands on your file will easily be able to transfer your data to their own PC.** After you create and confirm your password, click Save, then save the Windows Easy Transfer file to your external storage device.

Once again, this is a time for patience; we've seen the process take 12 hours or more on PCs that were packed to the rafters with files (especially ones that are large in size such as videos and photos). When Windows Easy Transfer is finished, you'll be reminded of the name of the Windows Easy Transfer file and where it's been saved, after which you can disconnect the external storage device from your old PC and connect it to your new one.

## Transfer Files to a New PC

After you connect the drive to your new PC, access it to find and open the file called *Windows Easy Transfer – Items from old computer*. Double-click the file and you'll see a reminder that only files—not settings—will be transferred and be prompted to enter your password (if you created one). Then a window just like the one shown in Figure 13-4 will appear, except the button at the lower right will say Transfer instead of Next.

If there are any items you transferred from your old PC but that you have since decided that you don't want to transfer to your new one, you can uncheck those items here via the same process described earlier. Once you're satisfied with your selections, choose Transfer and your files will begin transferring to the new PC. **Notice that you can't cancel the transfer once it's begun.** When the transfer is complete, you might want to put the external drive away for safekeeping in case you need to repeat the transfer in the future (or if you chose not to transfer all the files and need to transfer some more later).

---

■ **Tip**  It's also important to notice that after Windows Easy Transfer copies the files from your old PC, the originals are left intact. Therefore, before you sell, give away, recycle, or otherwise discard the old PC, you should take steps to ensure that its data can't be accessed by someone else. For more on this, see Chapter 14.

---

# Backup and Restore

If you want to get your files from an old Windows 7 PC to a new Windows 10 PC, you cannot use either File History or Windows Easy Transfer, because the former didn't yet exist in Windows 7 and Microsoft removed the latter from Windows 10. You can, however, transfer files between Windows 7 and Windows 10 via the Backup and Restore feature, which is common to both operating systems.

We taked about Backup and Restore briefly in Chapter 11 but didn't explore it in detail as it's not included in Windows 8.1 and File History is a better way of actually backing up your files in Windows 10. So for information on how to use Backup and Restore to back up your files on a Windows 7 PC, see http://windows.microsoft.com/en-us/windows/back-up-files#1TC=windows-7.

Once you've made the backup on your old Windows 7 PC, connect the drive holding the backup to your new Windows 10 PC, search for "backup" and run *Backup and Restore (Windows 7)*. Then choose *Select another backup to restore files from* (Figure 13-7), and you'll be able to access the backup to restore its files onto that PC.

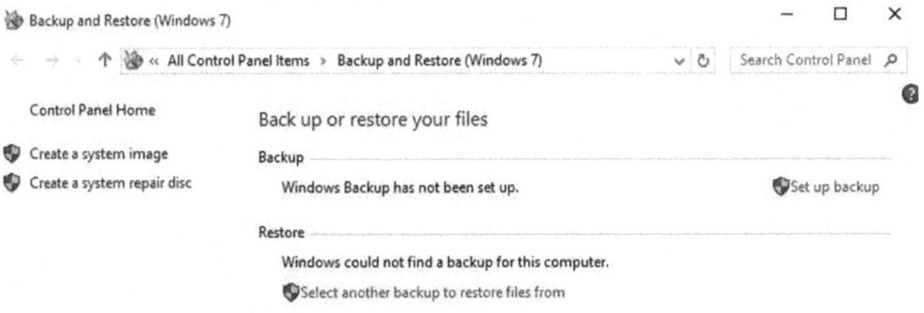

*Figure 13-7.* *Use Backup and Restore to transfer files from a Windows 7 PC to a Windows 10 PC*

■ **Tip** Be sure that you run the item labeled *Backup and Restore (Windows 7),* which will appear under the settings heading, not the one simply labeled *Backup and Restore,* which may appear first in the search results. The latter is an app from the Windows Store that won't be very helpful.

## WHAT ABOUT APPLICATIONS?

All of the methods discussed in this chapter will transfer files from one PC to another, but won't transfer the applications you use to create and/or organize those files such as Microsoft Word, iTunes, Quicken, and so on.

There are several third-party tools that purport to transfer not just files but also settings and applications from one PC to another, and do so across different versions of Windows (e.g., Windows 7 to Windows 10).

We can't vouch for their effectiveness, but two that might be worth checking out are:

LapLink PCmover Professional ($59) (the paid version of PC Mover Express discussed earlier in this chapter)

www.laplink.com/index.php/specialpages/Branded-PCmover-012014

EaseUS Todo PCTrans Pro 8.0 ($50)

www.easeus.com/pc-transfer-software/pctrans-pro.html#win10offer

(Laplink cites a 30-day money-back guarantee, while EaseUS offers a free trial version.)

# File Transfer via the Cloud

Last but not least, we should mention that if you sync and store files in the cloud with Microsoft's OneDrive or another online service such as Amazon, Dropbox, Google, iCloud, and so on, that can be a relatively easy way to get your files transferred over to a new PC.

Although features and procedures will vary by provider, in many cases simply logging into your cloud account on your new PC will automatically download all of your synced files to it. Although it may not eliminate the need to transfer files via one of the methods discussed in this chapter—you may not keep *all* of your files in the cloud—it may help to simplify the process.

# CHAPTER 14

■ ■ ■

# Properly Disposing of an Old PC

In the previous chapter we discussed two ways to copy files and folders from your personal data from an old PC to a new one: File History and Windows Easy Transfer.

Once you've transferred your personal data off an old PC, good file management practice dictates that the job isn't quite done yet. Chances are, you will dispose of that old PC in some way; you may plan to sell it, donate it to charity, hand it down to a friend or family member, or simply decide to leave it at the curb for recycling. Depending on which of these options you choose, you'll want to remove all of your personal data from the PC, but that isn't quite as simple as deleting your files and calling it a day. This is especially true if the PC will be sold, donated, or recycled. In these cases, in order to dispose of a PC safely, you need to take steps to minimize the chances that any of your deleted data can be recovered.

Why is this important? Because, as we know from earlier in this book, deleting files or folders in Windows doesn't necessarily make them go away permanently; it just makes them invisible to the operating system and then marks the disk space that they used to occupy as available for future use. Under normal circumstances, "deleted" data can easily be restored from the Recycle Bin, and even if you've disabled the Recycle Bin—or bypassed it by holding down SHIFT when you delete items—there are numerous free or inexpensive software programs available that can find and recover ostensibly deleted information with minimal time and effort.

The consequences of your personal information falling into the wrong hands can be quite serious (including identity theft), so to guard against this, it's very important to "wipe" the hard drive of any PC that you plan to get rid of. Wiping a hard drive involves erasing the data, overwriting the resulting free space one or more times with random information, then erasing it again. This process greatly minimizes the odds that whoever might come into possession of the PC will be able to successfully recover any of your personal data from it.

```
HOW WIPING A HARD DRIVE PROTECTS YOUR
PERSONAL DATA
```

To get a sense of how wiping a hard drive works, imagine that you wrote something in pencil (or erasable ink) on a piece of paper, and then erased what you wrote and threw away the paper. There's a good chance that someone who found that paper in the trash would be able to figure out much of what you'd wrote by looking at faint residual markings and/or indentations in the paper.

Now, imagine instead that after erasing your own writing, you wrote new words over it, then erased it again, then repeated that one, or two, or ten more times before throwing the paper away. Someone who came across *that* piece of paper would almost certainly not be able reconstruct anything meaningful from it, and even if they could, doing so would be a long and painstaking process.

To be clear, although wiping a hard drive doesn't provide a 100 percent guarantee that some personal data won't be recoverable, it makes the amount of effort required so high, and the odds of success so low, that most people wouldn't bother to try.

Fortunately, Windows offers a convenient way to "reset" a PC so that you can safely repurpose or dispose of it without leaving any personal data behind for someone to find.

# Resetting a Windows 8.1 PC

When you reset a PC in Windows, the following things happen:

- Your applications and personal data are deleted

- (Optional) Your hard drive is wiped

- A fresh copy of Windows gets reinstalled

- Any manufacturer or third-party applications or software that came with your PC are reinstalled

In a nutshell, resetting your Windows PC essentially returns it to the same "factory condition" it was in when you first took it out of the box. Considering how much junk software typically comes with PCs these days, this may not necessarily be a good thing, but it protects your data while also ensuring that the PC will be usable by the next owner (if there is one).

---

■ **Warning**   Be sure that you've transferred your personal data from a PC (e.g., made copies or backups) before beginning the reset process.

---

To kick off the reset process, type "reinstall" from the Windows 8 Start screen, then select *Remove everything and reinstall Windows*, as shown in Figure 14-1.

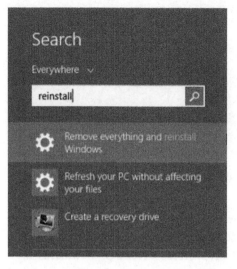

***Figure 14-1.*** *Search for "reinstall" to find the reset feature*

Next, find the *Remove everything and reinstall Windows* option and tap or click the *Get Started* button (Figure 14-2).

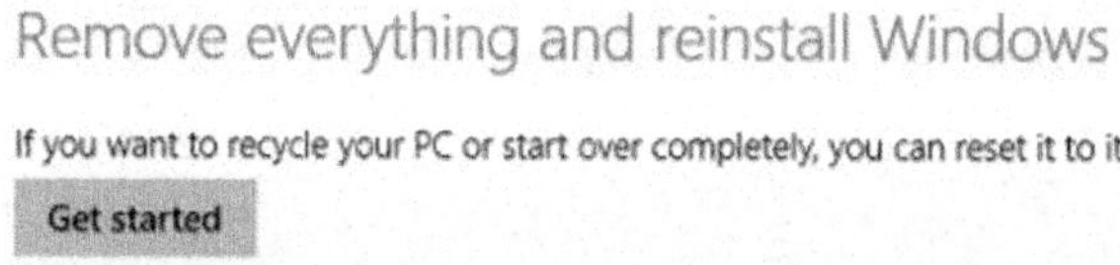

## Remove everything and reinstall Windows

If you want to recycle your PC or start over completely, you can reset it to its factory settings.

Get started

***Figure 14-2.*** *Click Get started under "Remove everything..." to kick off the reset process*

---

If you're on a battery-powered PC such as a laptop or tablet and aren't plugged into AC power, Windows will remind you to do that before proceeding any further. A reset can be a lengthy process, and draining your battery before it finishes can leave you with an unusable computer.

---

After a few moments of preparation, Windows will be ready to start the reset, unless it doesn't have all of the operating system files that it needs to perform the procedure. This is most likely if you installed Windows yourself, as opposed to having it preloaded on your computer. If Windows needs files, it will ask you to insert installation or recovery media, as shown in Figure 14-3. This is typically a DVD or USB flash drive that was either included with your PC or that you created when you first set up your PC.

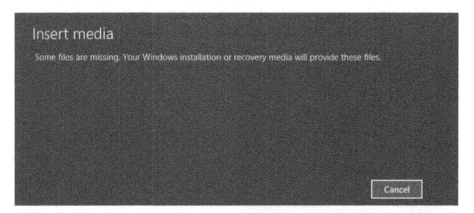

**Figure 14-3.** *If Windows needs files to complete the reset, it will ask you to provide them via a DVD or USB flash drive*

■ **Note** If your Windows 8.1 system didn't come with installation or recovery media, you may be able to create it by visiting http://windows.microsoft.com/en-us/windows-8/create-reset-refresh-media. This won't include manufacturer-specific software, however, so after using the recovery media you'll still need to download those things from the manufacturer's website.

Here's where it gets interesting. Next you'll be asked, "Do you want to fully clean your drive?" and given two choices: *Just remove my files* or *Fully clean the drive* (Figure 14-4).

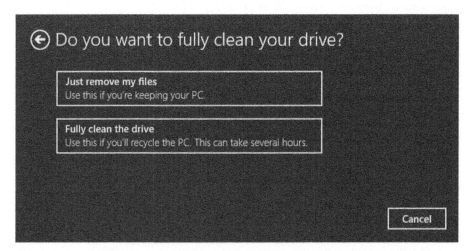

**Figure 14-4.** *Which option you choose will depend on what you plan to do with the PC*

If the PC will be staying within your household—for example, if you're handing it down to a child—the *Just remove my files* option is acceptable because it will delete your personal data from the computer (albeit not thoroughly enough to preclude potential recovery). But for any scenario in which the PC will no longer be under your control (sold, donated, recycled, etc.), *Fully clean the drive* is the appropriate choice. ("Clean" is Microsoft's term for "wipe".)

After you've made your choice, click the *Reset* button (Figure 14-5) and the process will proceed without any further input from you. The computer will restart several times. Be especially patient when you choose the clean option because it may take several hours to finish.

*Figure 14-5.* *This is the point of no return: click Reset to erase your data and return your PC to factory condition*

When the reset is complete, your PC will start up the same way it did when you first turned it on, ready to reuse, or if you chose the clean option, you can safely dispose of it.

It's important to reiterate that a reset returns your PC to its original factory condition, so if your PC is running Windows 8.1 but came with Windows 8, the reset will revert it to the latter operating system, after which you can repeat the Windows 8.1 upgrade.

## RESETTING A WINDOWS 10 PC

To reset a PC in Windows 10, search for "reset", choose Reset this PC, then click or tap the Get Started button located until Reset this PC. From this point, the process will be similar to that described earlier for Windows 8.1.

# An Alternate Drive Wiping Method

Windows' reset feature is handy because it lets you destroy your personal data without destroying the usability of the PC. Nevertheless, there are some scenarios in which a reset might not be an option. For example, the process we just outlined might fail for some reason, or you might not even be able to get into Windows to initiate it.

---

If you can't get into Windows on a Windows 8 or Windows 10 PC to do a reset, the USB recovery drive we mentioned earlier may let you start up your system and initiate a reset.

---

What if you have a pre-Windows 8 PC? Windows 7 PCs, for example, usually provide a factory reset option, but the process varies by manufacturer and almost never include a "wipe drive" option to allow for safe disposal.

If you have a Windows 7 PC that you want to wipe personal data from but still have a usable PC after the fact, the best way to accomplish this is to do the factory restore on the PC, then restart the system and use a utility that lets you wipe only the free space on a hard drive rather than the entire drive. Two such (free) utilities are BleachBit and Moo0 Anti-Recovery, available at http://bleachbit.sourceforge.net/download and http://www.moo0.com/software/AntiRecovery/, respectively.

## DBAN

If you can't do a Windows reset, a good fallback option to protect your data is to use third-party software to wipe the drive. One of the best choices is a relatively easy-to-use utility called DBAN, which you can download for free at www.dban.org/download. DBAN downloads as an ISO file (a disc image file format), so before you can use it you must burn the image to an actual CD or DVD. To do this, just put a blank disc in the drive, then double-click the ISO file and follow the steps.

---

To prevent inadvertent erasure of important data, be sure to disconnect any external storage devices (e.g., USB hard drives or Flash drives) from the computer before running DBAN.

---

To run DBAN, start the computer using the CD or DVD that you just created. To do this, when you first turn the computer on, look on the screen for a message telling you which key to press to bring up the boot menu (which lets you start from the disc rather than the system's hard drive). The boot menu key varies by manufacturer, but it's usually ESC, F2, or one of the keys in the range of F8 through F12. If you don't see a boot menu key listed when you turn your system on, restart it and take a closer look, as it can appear and disappear quickly. Otherwise, check the documentation for your system.

Once you've managed to summon the boot menu, highlight the CD/DVD drive (it may also be called the "optical drive"), press Enter, and within a few seconds you should see the screen shown in Figure 14-6.

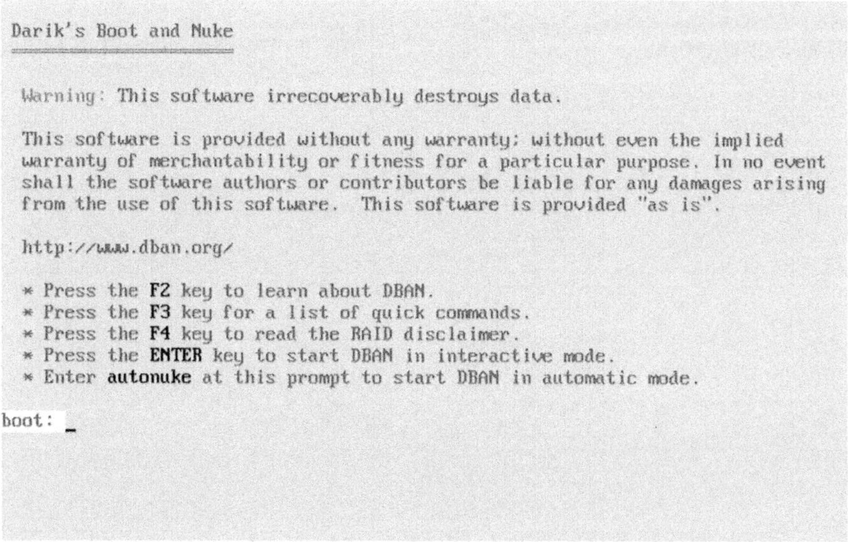

```
Darik's Boot and Nuke
═══════════════════════════

Warning: This software irrecoverably destroys data.

This software is provided without any warranty; without even the implied
warranty of merchantability or fitness for a particular purpose. In no event
shall the software authors or contributors be liable for any damages arising
from the use of this software. This software is provided "as is".

http://www.dban.org/

* Press the F2 key to learn about DBAN.
* Press the F3 key for a list of quick commands.
* Press the F4 key to read the RAID disclaimer.
* Press the ENTER key to start DBAN in interactive mode.
* Enter autonuke at this prompt to start DBAN in automatic mode.

boot: _
```

***Figure 14-6.*** *You'll see this screen if you successfully start your PC from a DBAN disc*

At this point, you have some choices to make. To keep things simple, you can simply type **autonuke** at the ***boot:*** prompt, and DBAN will automatically (and without asking you for confirmation) wipe every storage device that's inside or connected to your PC. DBAN's autonuke option overwrites your hard drive three times using the DoD (Department of Defense) short data destruction method. Alternately, you can press Enter to start DBAN in interactive mode, which lets you choose your own destruction method, which drives it will run on, and the number of times that it will run.

Regardless of whether you run DBAN in autonuke or interactive mode, while it's wiping your drive you'll see a screen similar to the one shown in Figure 14-7, telling you how long the wipe will take and how long until it's complete.

```
                        Darik's Boot and Nuke 2.2.8
───────────── Options ─────────────    ───────────── Statistics ─────────────
Entropy: Linux Kernel (urandom)        Runtime:        01:29:52
PRNG:    Mersenne Twister (mt19937ar-cok)  Remaining:   00:07:25
Method:  DoD Short                     Load Averages: 1.00 1.07 1.40
Verify:  Last Pass                     Throughput:    22830 KB/s
Rounds:  1                             Errors:        0


ATA Disk Windows (10) Tec F.FR 64GB FQBK67RT4N5K9ZJJQVCS
 [97.04%, round 1 of 1, pass 3 of 3] [blanking] [22830 KB/s]
```

*Figure 14-7.* *While wiping a drive, DBAN will report how much longer the process will take*

Speaking of that, when using DBAN, be prepared to wait a very long time. Depending on the method that you choose, the number of rounds, and the size of your hard drive, the process could take anywhere from many hours to many days. When it's all done, you'll see the screen shown in Figure 14-8, indicating that DBAN successfully wiped your drive and your PC is safe to dispose of. If you see something other than this screen, the wipe process failed for some reason, usually due to a hardware problem with the drive. In this case, see the next section, "As a Last Resort."

```
DBAN succeeded.
All selected disks have been wiped.
Hardware clock operation start date:  Tue Apr 28 16:32:30 2015
Hardware clock operation finish date: Tue Apr 28 18:04:03 2015

 * pass ATA Disk Windows (10) Tec F.FR 64GB FQBK67RT4N5K9ZJJQVCS

Press any key to continue..._
```

*Figure 14-8.* *DBAN has successfully wiped the drive*

## A COUPLE OF DBAN CAVEATS

Many thin-and-light laptops don't include optical drives, which will preclude you from using a DBAN disc on them. Although there's a way to put DBAN on a USB flash drive and start a PC with it, the process to do so can be intimidating to nontechnical people. If you want to take a crack at this, you'll find instructions at `http://www.pendrivelinux.com/install-dban-to-a-usb-flash-drive-using-windows/`, but a much easier option is to run DBAN via an external USB DVD drive, which you can buy online for under $25.

In addition, many modern PCs (both laptops and desktops) have a security feature called Secure Boot. It's designed to prevent someone from bypassing the internal hard drive and starting the system with a DVD or other external storage device. So you'll most likely need to disable this feature to use DBAN. The process to do so can vary by manufacturer, so consult your documentation or Google "disable secure boot" and/or "UEFI Legacy Boot" along with your PC's make and model. The following link discusses how to do this on HP systems: `support.hp.com/us-en/document/c03653226`.

Finally, DBAN only works on hard drives, not on SSD storage devices (Solid State Drives, which are often found in thin-and-light laptops and laptop/tablet hybrids). To wipe an SSD, use a utility provided by the SSD manufacturer. If you're not sure which company made the SSD, another option is Parted Magic, which can be purchased at low cost from `www.partedmagic.com`.

## As a Last Resort

Let's say that for whatever reason, reset isn't an option and DBAN won't run or doesn't wipe your drive successfully. If you want to dispose of a PC without worrying about whether your personal data might be accessible, your best remaining option is to physically destroy the drive.

A (relatively) simple way to do this is to remove the hard drive from the PC and use a powerful drill to bore several holes through it. Removing the hard drive can be easier said than done on some systems, especially on thin laptops where accessing it may require completely disassembling the computer.

But assuming that you can get to the drive to drill it, do it from the top where the label is (the bottom has a circuit board on the bottom that could go flying) and be sure to wear goggles to protect your eyes from debris. Drilling three or four holes in the drive is about as close as you can get to absolute assurance that any data it contained will be be safe from prying eyes.

# Index

## ▨ W, X, Y, Z

# Get the eBook for only $5!

Why limit yourself?

Now you can take the weightless companion with you wherever you go and access your content on your PC, phone, tablet, or reader.

Since you've purchased this print book, we're happy to offer you the eBook in all 3 formats for just $5.

Convenient and fully searchable, the PDF version enables you to easily find and copy code—or perform examples by quickly toggling between instructions and applications. The MOBI format is ideal for your Kindle, while the ePUB can be utilized on a variety of mobile devices.

To learn more, go to www.apress.com/companion or contact support@apress.com.

Printed by Printforce, the Netherlands